W9-BWZ-845

DISCARD

Princess Jellyfish 08

Akiko Higashimura

31333049357583

Episode 75
The Jellyfish
Princess in the Tower

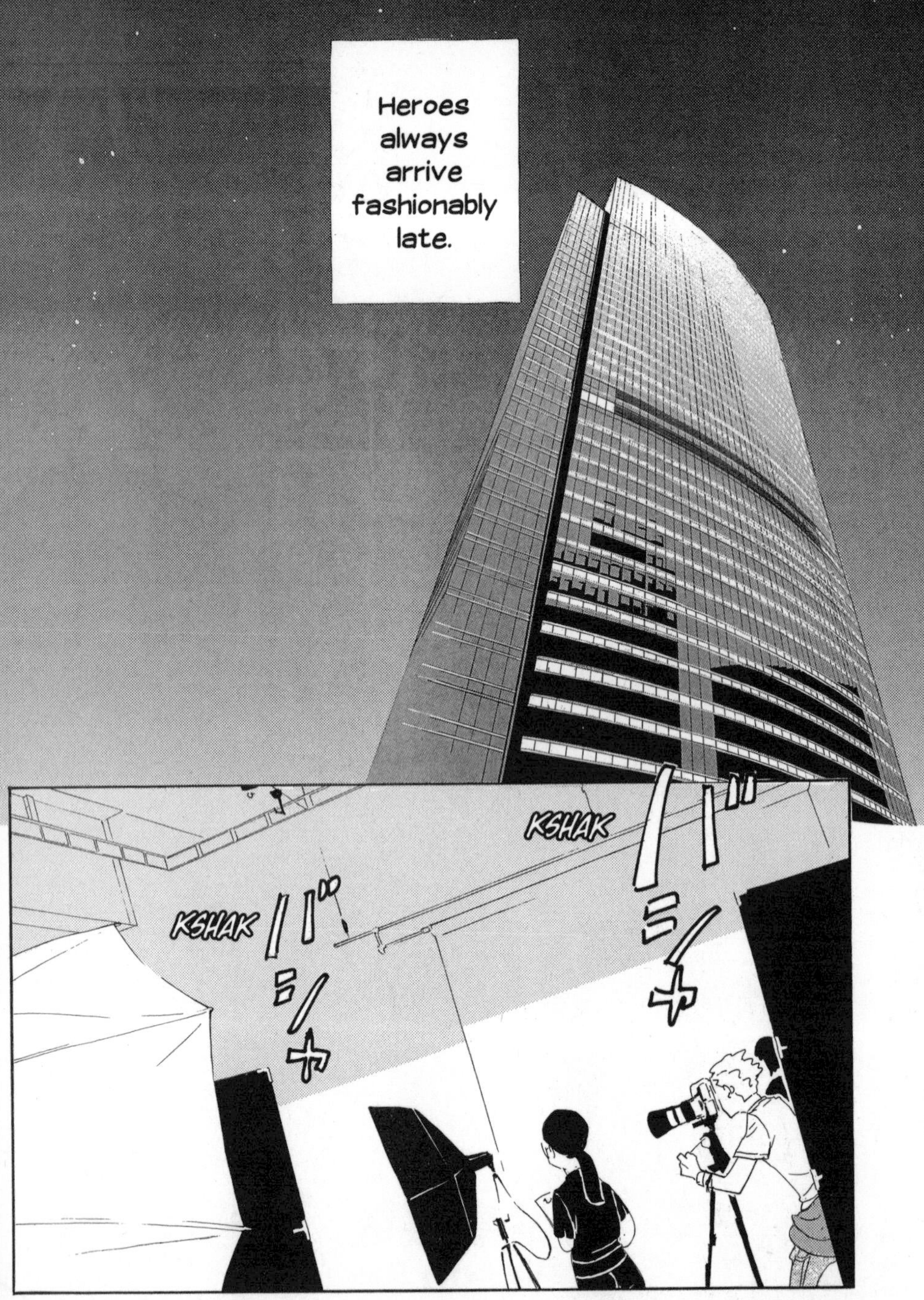
Heroes always arrive fashionably late.
KSHAK
KSHAK

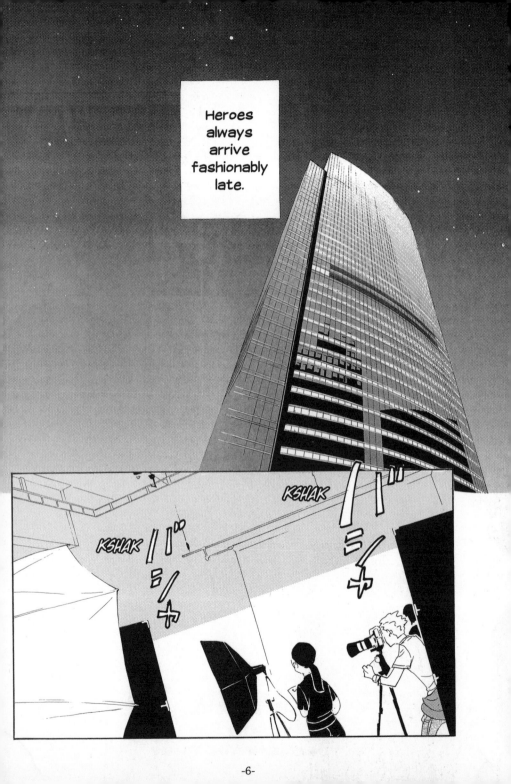

KSHAK
RATTLE RATTLE
OKAY! CHANGE TO THE NEXT ONE!!
FLUMP FLUMP
LET'S SEE, NEXT WE HAVE 18 PIECES FROM THE KNIT COLLECTION...
LET'S GO, SUE!
A LITTLE MORE WORK AND YOU'RE DONE!
clap

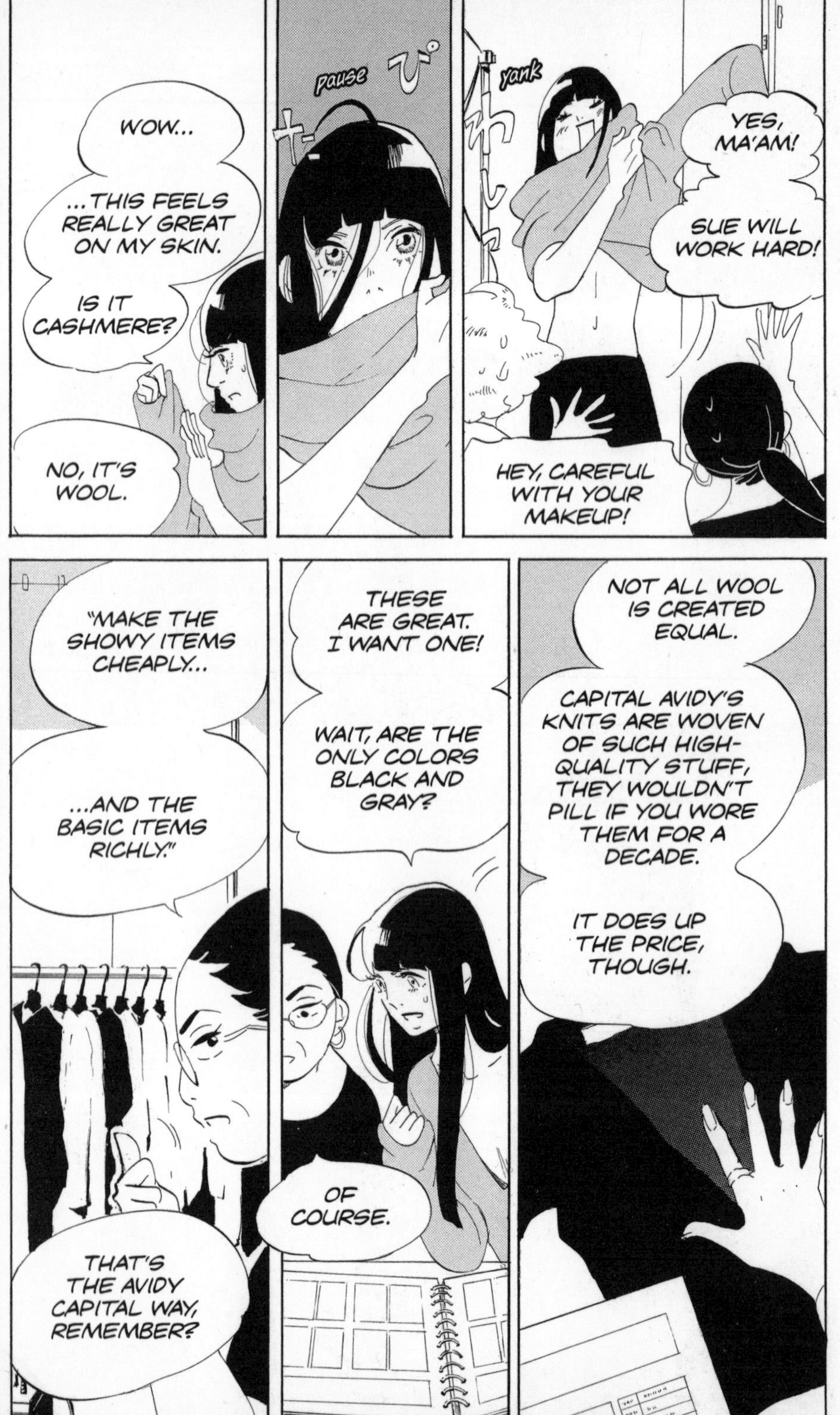
WOW...
...THIS FEELS REALLY GREAT ON MY SKIN.
IS IT CASHMERE?
NO, IT'S WOOL.
pause
ぴ
yank
YES, MA'AM!
SUE WILL WORK HARD!
HEY, CAREFUL WITH YOUR MAKEUP!
"MAKE THE SHOWY ITEMS CHEAPLY...
...AND THE BASIC ITEMS RICHLY."
THAT'S THE AVIDY CAPITAL WAY, REMEMBER?
THESE ARE GREAT. I WANT ONE!
WAIT, ARE THE ONLY COLORS BLACK AND GRAY?
OF COURSE.
NOT ALL WOOL IS CREATED EQUAL.
CAPITAL AVIDY'S KNITS ARE WOVEN OF SUCH HIGH-QUALITY STUFF, THEY WOULDN'T PILL IF YOU WORE THEM FOR A DECADE.
IT DOES UP THE PRICE, THOUGH.

...WAIT, YOU DIDN'T EVEN KNOW THAT?
S-SORRY! I'M JUST SO NEW!
Tee-hee!
Right, let's get started!!
...
...
UM...
...HERE?

I'M EATING DINNER HERE?

Personnel Change
Tsukimi Kurashita of the General Affairs Dept. is hereby transferred to the Archives Dept.
DA-DUN
FILE ROOM
creak
HELLO!
I'M TSUKIMI KURASHITA, THE NEW TRANSFER...
swivel
WELL, MY GOODNESS.
IT'S BEEN DECADES SINCE SOMEONE NEW WAS ASSIGNED HERE.
IT'S THAT ROOM?!
hmph
clack clack

prim
つーん
ER...
THANK YOU FOR DINNER...
pok
カパ

HUH.
IT'S CURRY.

munch
もそ…

ISN'T FAYONG-SAN GOING TO EAT?
O-OH, MAYBE SHE DOESN'T WANT TO EAT WITH SOMEONE LIKE ME...

ACTUALLY...
FAYONG-SAN ALWAYS GETS ASSIGNED TASKS LIKE THIS...
DOESN'T THAT BOTHER HER?
glance
チラ

OH...
THIS IS FISH CURRY, TOO...
A-A bone...!
MAYBE IN SINGAPORE, IT'S NORMAL TO HAVE FISH IN YOUR CURRY?
...
IS SOME-THING THE MATTER?
HMM?!

FISH CURRY.
I-I ATE IT WITH THE CEO.
HE, UM...
Um...
Um...
HE TOOK ME TO A SORT OF... INDIAN AREA...
V-VERY DELI-CIOUS...
INDIAN?

HE BOUGHT YOU FISH CURRY IN LITTLE INDIA?
UM.
YES.
"LITTLE INDIA" ...?
OH.
YES! FISH CURRY!
...
skrut
HUH?
ka-chak
HUH?
HUH?!
SLAM

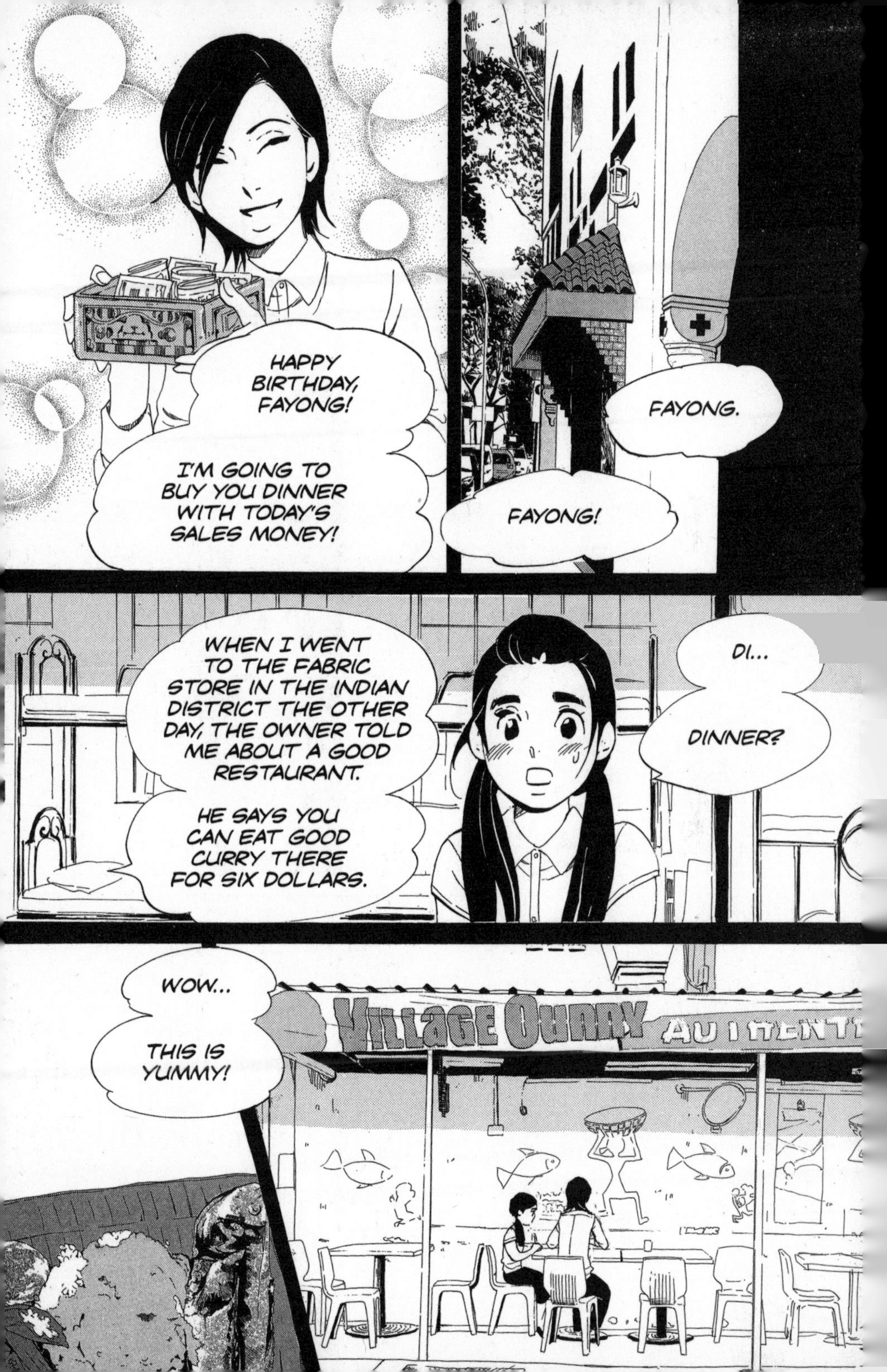
HAPPY BIRTHDAY, FAYONG!
I'M GOING TO BUY YOU DINNER WITH TODAY'S SALES MONEY!
FAYONG.
FAYONG!
WHEN I WENT TO THE FABRIC STORE IN THE INDIAN DISTRICT THE OTHER DAY, THE OWNER TOLD ME ABOUT A GOOD RESTAURANT.
HE SAYS YOU CAN EAT GOOD CURRY THERE FOR SIX DOLLARS.
DI...
DINNER?
WOW...
THIS IS YUMMY!
VILLAGE CURRY

IT'S GREAT!
YOU USUALLY HATE FISH, BUT EVEN YOU LIKE THIS, RIGHT?
YEAH!
munch
munch
IT'S SO DIFFERENT FROM THE CURRY AT THE ORPHANAGE!!
I'VE NEVER HAD FISH SO GOOD!
SINGAPORE WAS ORIGINALLY A FISHERMEN'S ISLAND, SO THE FISH HERE ARE GOOD.
IF WE WENT TO A RESTAURANT DOWNTOWN, THERE'D BE EVEN BETTER FISH!
NUH-UH.
I LIKE THIS BEST!
THIS FISH CURRY IS THE BEST IN THE WORLD!!
EVERYONE, I'D LIKE YOU TO MEET SOMEONE.

THIS IS AN OLD FRIEND OF MINE WHO'S DONATED A LOT OF MONEY TO THE ORPHANAGE.
HIS NAME IS MR. FISH.
PFFT!
プッ
MR. FISH! THAT'S A FUNNY NAME!
IS HE ENGLISH?
HE'S FISH CURRY.
giggle giggle
クス クス
HELLO THERE, KIDS.
I THINK I'M MEETING MOST OF YOU FOR THE FIRST TIME.
WHAT?

ME?
WHEN I TOLD MR. FISH ABOUT YOUR BAZAAR BOOTH...
...HE WAS VERY INTERESTED.
HIS SON DIED IN AN ACCIDENT SOME TIME AGO, YOU SEE.
WHEN HE SAW YOU, KAI, HE SAID YOU WERE THE SORT OF CLEVER CHILD WHO COULD INHERIT HIS BIG TRADING COMPANY.
KAI...
CONSIDER IT, WON'T YOU?

PARTHENON OF LOVE IS GONNA BE REPRINTED...
WOW!
da-dun
da-dun
TO PARTHENON OF LOVE'S REPRINTING!!
HUZZAH!!

THANK YOU, AYANO KONGO-RIKI!
thump
THANK YOU, PRINCESS'S BRUNCH!
AND THANK YOU, YOSHIKO HAMA!
Nwaah!
WHO IS THAT?!
YOSHIKO HAMA, 17-YEAR-OLD HEROINE OF PARTHENON OF LOVE! WHO ELSE?!
SHE FLIPPED OUT AND BOUGHT A FIRST-RUN COPY AT A USED BOOKSTORE IN JIMBOU.
WELL! I'M IMPRESSED YOU FOUND IT!
shing
FORGET YOSHIKO HAMA—LET'S TALK ABOUT MONEY.
gleam
stab
IN REAL TERMS, HOW MUCH CASH WILL THIS BRING IN?

THAT'S ...

THEY'RE PRINTING 20,000 COPIES, AND MY ROYALTIES ARE 10%, SO... LIKE ¥800,000, I GUESS?

*About $8,000 USD.

THAT'S SO LITTLE!!

shock
I CAN'T BELIEVE IT...
ALL WE CAN BUY WITH THAT IS A USED COROLLA!

shff
THE PUBLISHING INDUSTRY'S IN A SLUMP RIGHT NOW. MAKING THIS MUCH MONEY IS A MIRACLE, SRSLY
WHAT?!

I-I SEE...
EVEN 800,000 YEN IS MIRACULOUS...
DASH
GAAAAAH!
WHAT'S WRONG, MAYAYA?

ドドドドドド

SLUMP!

SLUMP!!

SLUMPS AND RECESSIONS!!

THUD THUD THUD

SLUMPS: STARRING RECESSIONS!

ドドドドドドド

THUD THUD THUD

WE'VE BEEN HEARING THOSE WORDS PRACTICALLY SINCE WE WERE BOOOOO-OOORN!!

WE CANNOT BE EXPECTED TO KNOW WHETHER WE ARE IN A SLUMP!

BECAUSE WE HAVE NEVER EXPERIENCED **GOOD** ECONOMIC TIMES!!

I MEAN NO DIS-RESPECT TO MEJIRO-SENSEI...

...BUT 800,000 YEN IS NO GOOD...!!

WE CAN'T SAVE TSUKIMI WITH 800,000 YEN!!

WAH! WAAA AAAAA AHH!!

MAYAYA! I'M BEGGING YOU, STOP WAILING!

The neighbors will call the police!

...

For goodness sake...
ガラ rattle
...
...
ストン… sit

800,000 YEN...

GOOD WORK, SUE!
YOU SAVED US!
clap
clap

AW!
SUE IS HAPPY TO HELP!
YOU WERE REALLY GOOD. I CAN'T BELIEVE YOU'RE A BEGINNER! I'M GOING TO ASK THE CEO TO GIVE YOU AN EXCLUSIVE CONTRACT WITH CAPITAL RIGHT AWAY!!

WHAAAT? THANK YOU, DIRECTOR!!
BY THE WAY...
zhoop
ずいっ
WHAT FLOOR IS THE CEO'S OFFICE ON?
SUE WANTS TO PAY HER RESPECTS!
FLOOR 35, OF COURSE!
THE TOP FLOOR, WITH A VIEW OF THE WHOLE BAY AREA...
じっ
stare
...
LISTEN UP, SUE.
LET ME GIVE YOU A WORD OF WARNING.
スッ
shff
USUALLY, I'M TOO PROFESSIONAL TO SAY THIS...
...BUT I THINK YOU REALLY WILL BE A GREAT MODEL, SO I'LL MAKE AN EXCEPTION.
OUR CEO MAY BE A GENIUS...
...BUT IF YOU LET THAT GENIUS STEAL YOUR HEART, YOU'LL RUIN YOUR CAREER.

YOU CAN SLEEP WITH HIM, BUT PLAY IT COOL.
HE HAS A BAD HABIT OF SLEEPING WITH EVERY TALENTED WOMAN AROUND HIM.
IT'S JUST THE WAY HE OPERATES.
BUT BE CAREFUL. I'VE SEEN PLENTY OF MODELS FALL FOR THE RICH, HANDSOME CEO...
...AND END UP FALLING TO PIECES.
tap

fwoom
sigh
KIKI.
WOULD YOU AT LEAST EAT A SALAD?
NO WAY.
I HAVE A SHOOT FIRST THING TOMORROW.
I CAN'T HAVE ANYTHING SALTY.
I SEE.
WANT TO ORDER FRUIT, THEN?
I'LL PASS.
I DON'T WANT TO END UP LIKE THE PIGGY PRINCESS.
PIGGY PRINCESS?
THE CEO'S NEW PET.
SHE'S ALL TINY AND ROLY-POLY...
klaf

AN UGLY LITTLE PIGGY.

HUH. HE HAS A PET PIG?

RICH PEOPLE REALLY ARE WEIRD.

YEP.

HE'S A WEIRDO.

ポイ toss

ゴクー gulp

ウィーン whmm

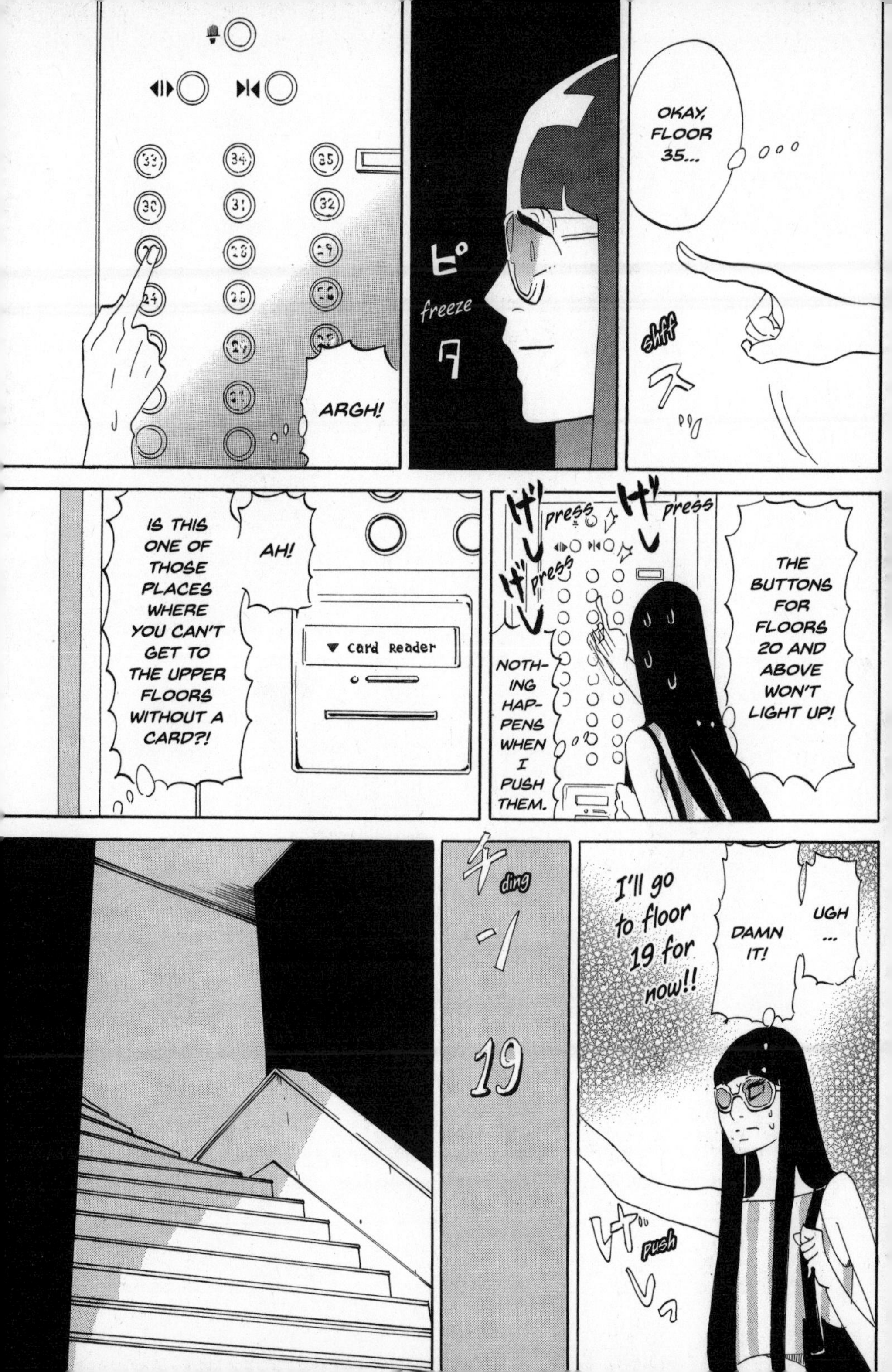

OKAY, FLOOR 35...
shff
ス
freeze
ピ
タ
ARGH!
THE BUTTONS FOR FLOORS 20 AND ABOVE WON'T LIGHT UP!
press
げ
press
げ
press
げ
NOTHING HAPPENS WHEN I PUSH THEM.
AH!
IS THIS ONE OF THOSE PLACES WHERE YOU CAN'T GET TO THE UPPER FLOORS WITHOUT A CARD?!
Card Reader
UGH ...
DAMN IT!
I'll go to floor 19 for now!!
push
ding
19

wheeze
wheeze
GAH!!
IT'S HARD TO CLIMB STAIRS IN A MAXI SKIRT!

WELL, ANYWAY... LOGICALLY SPEAKING...
huff huff
...THERE'S A GOOD CHANCE TSUKIMI IS ON ONE OF THESE UPPER FLOORS YOU NEED A CARD FOR.
huff huff
WHERE IS SHE?
THE CEO'S OFFICE, OR A HIDDEN ROOM INSIDE IT...?
...
HE HAS A BAD HABIT OF SLEEPING WITH EVERY TALENTED WOMAN AROUND HIM.
huff
NAH...
NO WAY...
IN HER CASE, WE SHOULD AT LEAST BE SAFE ON THAT FRONT...
So... I guess that's good...
35
huff
huff

35

I STILL NEED A CARD...

ZLIP

NOPE...
I'VE GOT A CLEAN-ING LADY HERE!!
GLEAM
HEY, YOU...
WHAT ARE YOU DOING HERE?
SHFF
HUH?!
flinch

ガッ
GRAB
HI THERE!
YOU'RE WORKING HARD, BABY.
WANNA COME HAVE SOME FUN WITH ME?
SORRY I SCARED YOU.
I'M ONE OF THE MALE MODELS.
THE NAME'S SU-ER, SUUTARO!
SLAM
YOU NAUGHTY BOY!
YOU SHOULDN'T TEASE AN OLD LADY LIKE THAT!
blush
I'VE BEEN JOGGING UP THE STAIRS ON THE CEO'S ORDERS!
IT'S TRADITIONAL FOR THE MALE AVIDY MODELS TO USE THIS LONG STAIRCASE TO EXERCISE, YOU KNOW?
OH, YOU DIDN'T KNOW?
RIGHT, I GUESS YOU WOULDN'T!

PHEW, I'M TIRED!
AND NOW I HAVE TO GO LISTEN TO HIM LECTURE ME!
SEE, I'VE GAINED WEIGHT LATELY...
YOU DON'T SAY... YOU SEEM PLENTY SKINNY TO ME. MODELS HAVE IT ROUGH!
BUT YOU STILL NEED TO EAT, OKAY?!
THANK YOU, HONEY.
I'D LIKE TO EAT YOUR HOME COOKING SOMETIME.
NOW, THEN!

WHICH WAY IS HIS OFFICE, AGAIN?
I have noooo sense of direction!
IT'S THAT BLACK DOOR AT THE END OF THE HALLWAY...
THANKS, HONEY!
HAVE A GREAT NIGHT!!
Dash!
pshooo

MY PRETTY FACE GOT ME BEHIND ENEMY LINES!
YESSSSS!
tmp tmp tmp tmp tmp
screech

ガチャ
KA-CHAK
DRIVE AROUND BACK.
WE'LL HEAD RIGHT TO THE HOTEL ON YONG SIAK STREET.
HEY.
I HAVE A SHOOT IN THE BAY AREA AT 5:00 AM.
I DON'T WANT TO OVERSLEEP. COULD YOU BOOK A ROOM?

...I HAVE WORK TONIGHT.

WITH THE LITTLE-PIGGY PRINCESS?

THERE IT IS.

THAT BLACK DOOR.

OKAY!

I'LL HIDE IN THE BATH-ROOM OR SOME-THING UNTIL—

KA-CHAK

shoop

ブルルル
brring brring
ビクッ
flinch
brring brring
ブルルル
HELLO.

I JUST GOT BACK.
IT'S GOING TO TAKE ME A BIT TO GET UP THERE. EVERYTHING OKAY?
WE'RE FINE, SIR.
THERE ARE NO PROBLEMS.
twitch
ピク
ピ
beep
...
...
YOUR NAME IS MISS FAYONG...
...RIGHT?
WANT TO MAKE A DEAL WITH ME?

rattle rattle
NOW, THEN.
TSUKIMI-SAN AND KURANOSUKE-SAN...
...HERE COMES THE MAN ON WHOM ALL FATES HANG.
HANAMORI TO THE RESCUE.

bang

vrrmmm
PLEASE TAKE ME CASINO.
I WANT LOT OF MONEY.

Book: Traveler's English

gleam
stab

Episode 76
The Monster of Singapore

They say that money can buy your way out of Hell...
Money from around the world comes here.
In *this* country, especially.
...but the living world is all about money, too.
MISS FAYONG...
WANT TO MAKE A DEAL WITH ME?

WHY DID YOU LIE JUST NOW?
THAT WAS HIM CALLING, RIGHT?
I SURE THINK ME SHOWING UP HERE COUNTS AS A PRETTY BIG PROBLEM.

WHY DID YOU SAY THERE WERE "NO PROBLEMS"?

SO, THEN.
clap
LET'S HAVE A CONSTRUCTIVE TALK!

I ONLY HAVE ONE DEMAND.

I WANT YOU TO GIVE BACK TSUKIMI.
I WANT TO TAKE HER BACK TO JAPAN RIGHT AWAY.

THAT'S IT.
SO...
...WHAT'S YOUR DEMAND?

MONEY?
OR OUR BRAND ITSELF?
NAH, YOU WOULDN'T WANT THAT.
I JUST SAW YOUR ENTIRE NEW LINE.
FRANKLY, IT'S ON A WHOLE OTHER LEVEL FROM THE CLOTHES WE'RE MAKING.
I ALMOST TOOK A PIECE FOR MYSELF WITHOUT THINKING.
I DON'T SEE HOW TSUKIMI'S DESIGNS COULD HAVE ANY INFLUENCE ON YOUR BRAND.
THE CEO'S ALREADY ESTABLISHED A PERFECT BUSINESS MODEL.
IT'S CRAZY THAT HE BROUGHT KNOW-NOTHING TSUKIMI ALL THE WAY HERE ON SOME WHIM!
pfff!
PERFECT?

NOTHING IN THIS WORLD IS PERFECT.
I'M GOING TO DO YOU A FAVOR.
I'LL SHOW YOU WHAT THE JOB OF SELLING CLOTHES IS REALLY LIKE.
HELLO, IS THIS NISHA-SAN?
IT'S JIJI...
SORRY TO CALL YOU AT WORK.

UM...
REMEMBER THE DYED ONE-PIECES NO ONE ORDERED AT THE EXHIBITION?
IF WE WANTED TO MAKE SOME OF THOSE, HOW MUCH WOULD YOU CHARGE TO SEW THEM...?
SAY WHAT?
OH, YA MEAN THE VENOMOUS JELLIES.
SURE, BUT WHAT'S UP? I THOUGHT YA QUIT THE BIZ?
OH, UM, I JUST WANTED TO ASK.

LEMME SEE...
WELL, THEY'RE A LOT EASIER THAN THE STUFF FROM BEFORE...
I RECKON WE CAN DO 'EM FOR 20,000 YEN* A POP.
Depends on how many ya order, though...

*About $200 USD.

WOULD THAT MAKE THE RETAIL PRICE...
...ABOUT 35,000 YEN** EACH?
YEAH, SOUNDS RIGHT.

OH, HEY.
YA KNOW YA'D HAVE TO DYE 'EM AT HOME, RIGHT?
IF YA WANT OUR FACTORY TO DYE 'EM, 20,000 YEN WON'T CUT IT.

**About $350 USD.

OH... WHAT?
I SEE ...
THAT MAKES SENSE ...
YER GROUP CAN DO TEN OR SO ON YER OWN, RIGHT?
IF WE ADDED THE LACE AND PEARLS OURSELVES, TOO, WOULD THAT MAKE IT A LITTLE CHEAPER?
A LITTLE, ANYWAY...
BUT WHAT'S GOIN' ON?

WHO'S GONNA BUY TEN DRESSES YA COULDN'T EVEN SELL AT AN EXHIBITION?
AND WHERE WOULDJA SELL 'EM?
ROADSIDE SALES AIN'T GONNA WORK, YA KNOW.

...
WHERE SHOULD WE SELL THEM?
HUH?
WHERE DO YOU THINK OUR CLOTHES...
...WOULD SELL WELL?

HOW THE HELL SHOULD I KNOW?!
I'M INDIAN!
AND ANYONE WHO KNEW WHERE THEIR CLOTHES'D SELL WOULD BE A FINANCIAL GENIUS!
RIGHT ...
...I SEE...
GOT IT. THANK YOU.
clunk
チーン
...
800,000 YEN...

"LITTLE-PIGGY PRINCESS" IS QUITE THE NICKNAME.
WHO WERE YOU TALKING ABOUT?
THAT GIRL FROM JAPAN WHO LOOKS LIKE A CHILD.
BUT YOU ALREADY KNEW THAT.
ENOUGH WITH THIS PATHETIC JEALOUSY, KIKI.
カッ blush
JEALOUSY?!
WHY SHOULD I BE JEALOUS OF A GIRL LIKE—
YOU MAY WEAR CLOTHES SHE DESIGNED SOMEDAY, YOU KNOW.
HA!
NO WAY CAN A PATHETIC GIRL LIKE THAT DESIGN COUTURE LINE CLOTHES.

I FIGURED YOU WERE STARTING UP A KIDS' BRAND OR SOMETHING.

NO, EVEN THAT'S TOO MUCH FOR HER. MAYBE CLOTHES FOR **PETS**.

KIKI.

FIRST-RATE MODELS SHOW DESIGNERS THE UTMOST RESPECT AND GRATITUDE.

EXCUSE ME?

"DESIGNER"?

SHE'S A NEWBIE WHO HASN'T EVEN DEBUTED YET.

OH, SHE'S ALREADY MADE HER RUNWAY DEBUT.

WHICH RUNWAY, EXACTLY?

IT WAS SOME CHEAP JAPANESE CASUAL SHOW, WASN'T IT?!

JAPANESE, YES.

AND IT WAS SMALL, BUT IT WAS A FULL-FLEDGED, HIGH-QUALITY HAUTE COUTURE SHOW.

SHE'S MY SUDDEN, UNEXPECTED...

...MONEYMAKING TOOL?

NO...

CASINO
...SHE'S LADY LUCK.
clack
fwip
NOW, THEN...
WHOM WILL LADY LUCK SMILE UPON TODAY?

shff
THAT WOULD BE ME!
twirl twirl
ta-dah
THE ONLY LUCK I HAVE IS GOOD!
Hanamori-san is pumped up about his rare overseas trip.
SO, LET'S SEE HOW MANY BENZES I CAN EARN WITH NISHA'S 100,000 YEN...*
Chips, please!
*About $1,000 USD.
IT'S TIME...
plunk
...FOR BATTLE!!

flip
SHEESH...
HOW LONG DO I HAVE TO STAY HERE?
FAYONG-SAN IS GONE, TOO...
WHAT...
WHAT DO I DO IN HERE?
THERE ARE LOTS OF BOOKS, SO MAYBE I'LL READ SOMETHING.
THEY'RE PROBABLY ALL IN ENGLISH, THOUGH...
NNGH...
MAYBE HE'LL HAVE SOMETHING ON THE SEA CREATURES OF SINGAPORE...
HMM?
2010
2011
THESE ARE...
...COMPANY RECORDS...?
flip

WOW...
THEY MAKE PRETTY NICE BOOKS...
RZPV 2000
RZPV 2001
RZPV 2002
RZPV
I WONDER IF THESE GET USED AT JOB FAIRS...
THERE'S ONE FOR EVERY YEAR SINCE 2000...
...
パッ
flip
It began with the White Shirt.

UGH, ENG-LISH...
"IT... BEGAN..." BEGAN? OH, BEGIN? AND HERE'S "WHITE SHIRT" ...
I THINK IT SAYS "IT BEGAN WITH A WHITE SHIRT" ...
...MAYBE?
HUH?
BUT...
THIS...
...ISN'T AN AVIDY SHIRT.
"F"...
DID THIS COMPANY ...
...START OUT AS A SHIRT STORE?
I'll start with an earlier book.
パラ
flip
OH!
THIS ONE, TOO...
It began with
White Shirt.
AND THIS ONE...
...AND THIS ONE...
ALL OF THEM ...
Oh!
はっ

EVERYONE WEARS WHITE SHIRTS HERE.
PUT THIS ON, PLEASE.
I...
I SEE...
SO THIS MEANS... I-IT'S ONE OF THOSE THINGS?
LIKE...
LIKE HOW SOMEONE JOINING THE YOMIURI GIANTS MIGHT WEAR A UNIFORM WITH THE OLD DESIGN FROM THE *OH AND NAGASHIMA* AGE...
A COMPANY LOYALTY THING...?
GIANTS 3
Not even close.

WHEW...
BIG COMPANIES ARE REALLY SOMETHING ELSE...

MR. CEO...

...WHAT DO YOU THINK I CAN DO...
...IN A COMPANY LIKE THIS?

...
WHERE ARE YOU PLANNING TO TAKE ME?
diiing
Basement Level 3?

vwurr

WHAT IS THIS PLACE...?
IT'S DARK!
rrrrumble
ズォオオオ
H-HEY!
YOU'RE NOT TRYING TO LOCK ME IN AN UNDER-GROUND CELL, ARE YOU?!
はしっ grab
カツ clack
THIS WAY.
カッカッカッ clack clack clack
キョロ glance
キョロ glance
WE'RE HERE.
ピ… beep
ウィーン… vwwrr

ARE...
ARE THESE ...
...ALL...
...CLOTHES ?
IT'S OVERSTOCK FROM BOTH CAPITAL AND LITTLE.
OVER-STOCK?
THIS MUCH?
WOW... THAT'S A SHOCKER...
I JUST ASSUMED YOU WERE MANAGING TO PRODUCE ONLY WHAT YOU COULD SELL...
GAH!
whmp

THIS ONE IS...

...A SUPER-EXPENSIVE KNIT LIKE THE ONE I JUST WORE...

バッ snatch

AVIDY

WHAT WILL YOU DO WITH THESE?

PUT THEM ON A SALE? SEND THEM TO OUTLETS?

WE'LL BURN THEM.

WE'LL BURN THEM.
ALL OF THEM.
...
YOU'RE KIDDING.
EVERYONE IN THE INDUSTRY DOES IT.
BUT ALL THE BRANDS HAVE OUTLET STORES!
THINK ABOUT IT— THERE ARE PLENTY THAT DON'T.
IF WE SLAPPED SALES TAGS ON ALL OUR LEFTOVER STOCK AND SOLD IT AT HALF PRICE...
...THOSE CUSTOMERS WOULD NEVER BUY OUR CLOTHES AT RETAIL PRICE AGAIN, WOULD THEY?

YOU AND THE PUBLIC ARE BEING FOOLED.

THESE DAYS, OUTLETS MOSTLY SELL "FACTORY OUTLET" GOODS.

"FACTORY OUTLET"?

MADE-FOR-OUTLET PRODUCTS.

OUTLETS STOCK LARGE NUMBERS OF GOODS MADE AT LOW COST FOR THE SOLE PURPOSE OF BEING SOLD AT OUTLETS.

...
HOLY CRAP.
THIS IS CRAZY...
YOU REALIZE YOU MIGHT AS WELL BE BURNING MONEY?
...
THE CHINESE MONSTER...
DO YOU KNOW THE MONSTER WHO APPEARS IN CHINESE LEGEND?
THE ONE CALLED HUNDUN.
IT ATE AND ATE, BUT NO MATTER HOW MUCH MEAT OR FISH IT ATE, IT WAS STILL HUNGRY.
LEGEND HAS IT THAT HUNDUN EVENTUALLY ATE EVERYTHING IN THIS WORLD...
...AND WHEN THERE WAS NOTHING LEFT TO EAT...

...IT ULTIMATELY ATE ITS OWN TAIL.

HUNDUN ENDED UP EATING ITSELF.

WE ARE JUST LIKE THAT MONSTER.

I BET, IN THE END, THERE WILL BE NOTHING LEFT.

EVERYONE, I APOLOGIZE...
...FOR CALLING YOU ALL HERE SO SUDDENLY.
WHY ARE YOU SPEAKING SO FORMALLY, JIJI-SAMA?
gulp
I'M NOT WATCHING THE *AIBOU* MOVIE WITH YOU AGAIN.
You showed me that thing six times.
NO...
THAT'S NOT IT. I WANTED TO CONSULT WITH YOU...
UM...
IT'S ABOUT MEJIRO-SENSEI'S 800,000 YEN IN ROYALTIES.
OH...
OKAY ...
IF...IF MEJIRO-SENSEI REALLY WANTS TO, UM... USE IT FOR AMAMIZUKAN ...
SHE'S BEEN SAYING ALL ALONG THAT SHE DOES.
YEAH, SHE TOLD US TO USE IT TO RESTORE AMAMIZUKAN.
Yep, yep.

THAT'S... TRUE. SHE SAYS IT'S ALL RIGHT TO USE IT.
SO... WELL ...
I HAVE A SUGGES- TION...
HOW ABOUT WE USE THE MONEY ON...
... CLO —
WHAT?! YOU HAD BETTER NOT SUGGEST ANOTHER FASHION SHOW!
I'M NOT PLAYING SEAM- STRESS AGAIN!
BE QUIET, BOTH OF YOU.
NO, THAT'S NOT IT...
I WANT TO USE THE MONEY ON CLOTH—
I DON'T WANT TO MAKE CLOTHES ANY- MORE!!
HMPH!
HAVE YOU FORGOTTEN THOSE HELLISH DAYS, JIJI- SAMA?!
WE WORKED SO HARD, WE WERE FORCED TO SEW ON PEARLS WITH THE BLOOD STILL RUNNING DOWN OUR HANDS FROM HAVING STABBED OURSELVES WITH PINS SO MANY TIMES, AND YET NOT ONE OF THOSE DRESSES SOLD AT THAT "EXHIBITION" AFFAIR!
ALTHOUGH THE SHAGGY- HAIRED HUMAN TRAFFICKER DID BUY TSUKIMI.
NO... THAT'S NOT IT...
HOW ABOUT WE USE THE MONEY...

...TO...
...BUY CLOTHES?
...
WHAT?
I MEAN... WELL...
WHY NOT TAKE THAT 800,000 YEN AND... UM... ALL BUY...
bloop

...PROPER, WELL...
...E-EXPENSIVE CLOTHES?
ポカーン
GAPE

*About $300 and $500 USD, respectively.

JIJI-SAMA...?
WHAT...
...ARE YOU...
...SAYING?
shff
スッ
L-LISTEN...
IT'S...
UM, EVEN *I* DON'T REALLY KNOW, BUT...
IT'S JUST...

...I WANT TO SELL THOSE ONE-PIECES AFTER ALL, TO HELP TSUKIMI-DONO...

BUT I HAVE NO IDEA WHERE WE SHOULD SELL THEM...

...AND WHEN I THOUGHT ABOUT WHY I HAD NO IDEA, I REALIZED...

I...
I DON'T KNOW THIS BECAUSE I'VE NEVER BOUGHT CLOTHES FROM A DECENT SHOP BEFORE.

SO BEFORE WE SELL OUR CLOTHES...
...FIRST...
...I THOUGHT WE SHOULD USE THIS MONEY TO BUY SOME CLOTHES.
OUR-SELVES.

TRIPLE SIXES!!

DA-DUN

whistle

swish

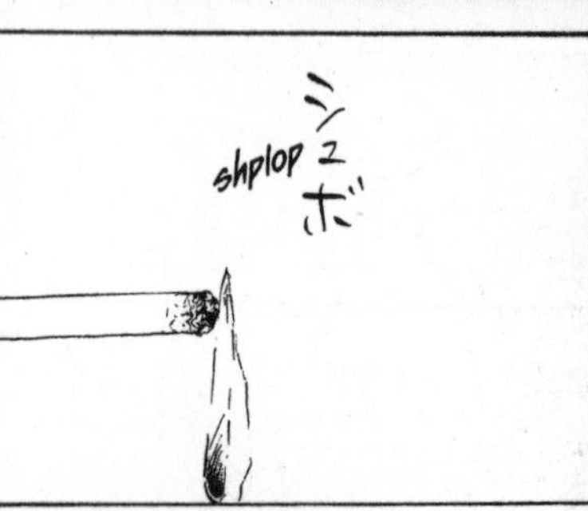

I BLEW 100,000 YEN IN UNDER A MINUTE...

Puff... フー...

Money makes the world go round.

You spend money to make more money.
Round and round it goes...
...like the monster eating its own tail.
There's only one way to stop the cycle.
MISS FAYONG.
I GET WHAT YOU WANT NOW.
YOU WANT TO STOP DOING THIS, DON'T YOU?
THAT'S WHY YOU SHOWED ME THIS, RIGHT?

I'm the only one in the world who can do it.
YOU WANT ME TO STOP HIM, DON'T YOU?

twirl
twirl
スタッ
ta-dah

Episode 77
Casino Royale

It's only a few minutes now until I retrieve the princess from the tower.
YOU WANT ME TO STOP HIM, DON'T YOU?
I'M AN OUTSIDER, NOT A PART OF YOUR COMPANY...
IN FACT, I'M PART OF YOUR COMPANY'S CUSTOMER BASE— A JAPANESE PERSON. SO FOR YOU TO SHOW THIS TO ME AND TELL ME YOUR SECRETS...
YOU KNOW, MISS FAYONG?
YOU...

...ARE A MORE RESPECTABLE PERSON THAN I THOUGHT.

SO...

...HOW ABOUT YOU TELL ME WHERE TSUKIMI IS?

I'LL TAKE TSUKIMI BACK TO JAPAN...

...AND THERE, WE'LL CREATE THE KIND OF BRAND THAT ONLY **WE** CAN.

THEN WE'LL SUCCEED USING TOTALLY DIFFERENT METHODS FROM HIS...

...AND I'LL FRIGGIN' **CRUSH** THIS STUPID COMPANY.

brring brring
プルルルル
HUH?!
HELLO, KURANO-SUKE-SAN?
GREET-INGS.
LIVE, FROM SINGAPORE... ***IT'S HANAMORI.***

... YOU'RE ...
... HERE ?
YES.
I ARRIVED AT THE AIRPORT TWO HOURS AGO.
QUICK AS HE ARRIVED, HE BECAME PENNILESS IMMEDIATELY ...
...I'M HANAMORI, AND THIS IS MY STORY.
KURANO-SUKE...
...I'M GOING TO CUT TO THE CHASE.
PLEASE LEND ME MONEY.
WHOA ... ...
WHY ARE YOU CALLING OUT OF NOWHERE AND SAYING THIS CRAP ?!
I'M IN THE CASINO AT MARINA BAY SANDS RIGHT NOW.
PLEASE COME, AND BRING MONEY.
CASINO ?!
YOU BLEW ALL YOUR MONEY AT A CASINO?!

YES, EXACTLY. BUT THE GAME HAS ONLY JUST BEGUN.
DON'T WORRY. ALL I HAVE TO DO IS WIN IT BACK, AND EVERYTHING'S GOLDEN.
That sounds like a load of crap...
...BUT HAVING SOMEONE ELSE ON MY SIDE IS A GOOD THING IN THIS SITUATION.
OKAY.
I'LL BE THERE IN 30!
bip
ピ
COME ON!
WE'RE OUT OF TIME, MISS FAYONG.
I HAVE TO GET TSUKIMI OUT OF HERE BEFORE HE—KAI—GETS BACK.
...
CAN I ASK YOU ONE THING?
WHAT IS YOUR...
...RELATIONSHIP WITH TSUKIMI?

HUH?!
ME?
I'M...
...HER...
...
grit
...LOVER, OF COURSE.
WHAT?
Here we go.
SHE'S MY FIANCÉE, ACTUALLY.
Time for an all-or-nothing gamble...

...to get back the princess.

MY DAD'S A FAMOUS POLITICIAN BACK IN JAPAN.

AND SINCE I'M HIS SUCCESSOR, I CHOSE HER FOR MY BRIDE.

GIRLS LIKE THAT ARE PERFECT FOR A POLITICAL FAMILY.

OH...

I SEE...

phew

ほっ

ピクッ

twitch

WAIT.

DOES SHE...

...FEEL LIKE THAT ABOUT HIM...?
YOU CAN SLEEP WITH HIM, BUT PLAY IT COOL.
WHOA.
BEING IN LOVE WITH A CEO WHO GOES AFTER ALL HIS OWN MODELS...
THAT'S A PRETTY HARSH OLD STORY.
But I've gotta take advantage of those womanly feelings!
HERE'S THE THING, THOUGH...
I THINK TSUKIMI HAS FALLEN FOR KAI.
flinch
ビクッ
THAT'S WHY I JUMPED ON A PLANE TO SINGAPORE.
SO LET'S HURRY.
NOW'S OUR ONLY CHANCE.
clack clack

...
SHFF
THE FILE ROOM ON THE 35TH FLOOR.
YOU CAN USE THIS CARD IN THE ELEVATOR TO GET TO THE UPPER FLOORS.
shoop
!!
WHOA!
fwish
WHAT?!
SHOULD I REALLY...
EVEN BELIEVE YOU?
YEAH.
I PROMISE YOU.
diiing
ONE DAY, I'LL CRUSH HIM AND THIS COMPANY.

AND WHEN THAT HAPPENS, I'M SURE HE'LL RETURN TO YOU.
vwwrr
SHOVE

SPEND TONIGHT WITH ME.
OR ELSE I'LL TELL PEOPLE ABOUT US.
...
THE WHOLE COMPANY KNOWS ABOUT US.
I MEAN TELL PEOPLE OUTSIDE THE COMPANY.
A FEW TWEETS FROM ME, AND BEFORE LONG, THE WHOLE WORLD WILL KNOW.
AND IF YOU TRY TO FIRE ME, I'LL TELL THE TABLOIDS ALL ABOUT OUR SEX LIFE.
ding

35
チン
ding
...
GOOD GRIEF...
fwoosh
プシュー
35
fwoosh
プシュー

DASH
BEEP
THERE IT IS!
THIS MUST BE IT.
KA-CHAK
...
TSUKI ...
sneak
...MI...?

くかー
ZZZZ
!!!
SHE...
SHE'S ASLEEP!
ぐぉー
SNORE
I... RISKED MY LIFE...
...TO MAKE IT TO THE TOP OF THIS TOWER...
...AND THIS FOUR-EYED PRINCESS IS JUST DROOLING AWAY!
HEY!
ぴくっ
FLINCH
WAKE UP, TSUKIMI!
MRMPH?
I SAID WAKE UP!

KURA...
...NO ...?
...SUKE ...
...SAN ...?
IN THE FLESH.
GRAB
HWA ...?!
I CAME TO GET YOU!
THONK
SO WAKE THE HELL UP!

OKAY.
LET'S GO.
YANK
WHA-WHA...?
WE'RE GETTING OUT OF HERE!!
STOMP STOMP STOMP
YEE!
YEEE-EEP!
STOMP
STOMP
RUN FASTER, YOU CLUMSY PRIN-CESS!
GOTTA GO RESCUE ANOTHER PRINCESS ON OUR WAY OUTTA TOWN...
I'M SORRY?
ANOTHER ONE?!
OHO!
SCREECH
YOINK
I'LL BE TAKING THIS!

all alone
KURA-NOSUKE-SAN'S TAKING FOR-EVER.
HOW MUCH LONGER?
STILL...
THANK GOOD-NESS THE COFFEE'S FREE.
THIS IS A GEN-EROUS CASINO ...
RIGHT.
I'LL DRINK LOTS.
beep
AH! THERE HE IS!
HANA-MORI-SAN!
huff
huff
HMM?

DARN IT! YOU ALREADY RESCUED HER?
BUT I HAD A SPECIAL PLAN TO CHARTER A HELICOPTER WITH THE MONEY I WON HERE AND SPIRIT HER AWAY FROM THE ROOF OF THE BUILDING, HOLLYWOOD-STYLE!
YOU LOST ALL THE MONEY YOU HAD!
Graaah!
EXCUSE ME, SIR.
I'M SORRY, BUT WE DON'T ADMIT ANYONE UNDER 20.
Passport, please.
WHAT?
YOU DON'T?!
It's fine, though, since I am 20!
WAIT, TSUKIMI, HOW OLD ARE YOU?
N-NINETEEN...
WAIT, REALLY?! AN OTAKU'S AGE REALLY IS UNIDENTIFIABLE!!!
WE DO HAVE A SPACE WHERE SHE CAN STAY, IF YOU'D LIKE...
YOU DO?!
SOUNDS GREAT! WHERE IS IT?!
THIS WAY.
DA-DUN
Kid's Club

KID'S ...
... CLUB ...?
She thinks I'm a grade-schooler with braids!
OHOHO.
I LIKE IT.
IT HAS A STRICT POLICY OF ONLY LETTING THE KIDS LEAVE WITH THEIR PARENTS...
PLUS A LOCKED GATE...
da-dun
EVEN KAI WON'T FIND YOU IN THIS PLACE!
OKAY, TSUKIMI, YOU WAIT HERE!
WHAT?!
I'LL BE BACK IN HALF AN HOUR!
I'M GOING TO MAKE AT LEAST ENOUGH FOR OUR PLANE FARE BACK HOME.
NOW YOU BE GOOD, KIDDO!
COME ON.
smile
WANT TO DRAW SOME PICTURES WHILE YOU WAIT?
Was that handsome man your brother? You don't look anything alike.
...
STRIDE

NOW, THEN.
LET'S SEE HOW MUCH I CAN MAKE IN HALF AN HOUR...
TIME FOR ME TO STRUT MY STUFF.
chak
チャッ
THIS IS THE TABLE I LOST AT, BY THE WAY.
shing
キリッ
pause
glance
チラッ

grin
hmm
I THINK I'LL BET HERE.
SOMEHOW I GET THE FEELING SHE'LL LET ME WIN.
WHAT?
BUT I'M SO MUCH HANDSOMER...
So why did I lose before?
SHE PROBABLY LIKES YOUNGER MEN.
THE CUTE TYPE.
fa la la
fwish
fwish
AW, THAT'S NOT FAIR.
HMM...
SO, I JUST HAVE TO BET ON THE NUMBERS THAT'LL COME UP ON THE DICE.
OKAY, GOT IT.
This payout is 5:1, and this one is 10:1.
YOU'RE QUICK ON THE UPTAKE.
chak
clink
I DID IT!
WOW.

YAY!
scoot
HEY.
YOU'RE BETTING LIKE YOU'RE SCROOGE, KURANO-SUKE-SAN.
NO, I'M NOT. I JUST TURNED 5,000 YEN INTO 10,000 YEN!*
I'LL SHOW YOU HOW A REAL MAN DOES IT.
HUH?!

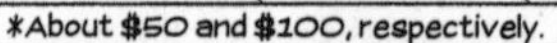
*About $50 and $100, respectively.

NO, STOP! CALM DOWN!
YOUR EYES HAVE GONE ALL WEIRD...
blaze
blaze
blaze
GRAB
WAH!
SMACK

IT'LL BE...
...TRIPLE SIXES THIS TIME!!

clink

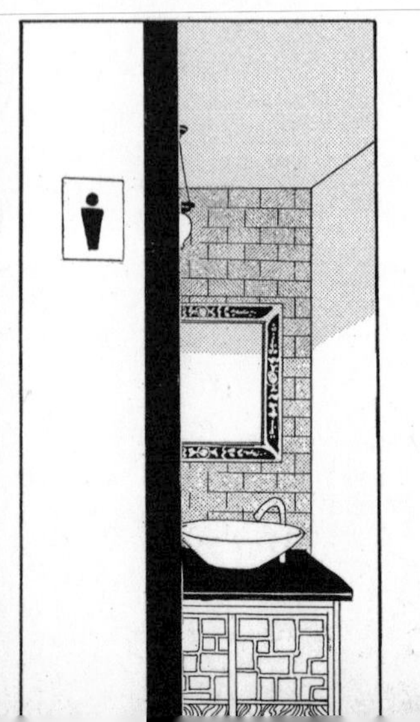

ARE YOU ANGRY, KURANO-SUKE?
YOU BET I AM.
YOU TOOK MY NEW 10,000 YEN...
...AND TODAY'S 50,000 YEN-WAR FUND, AND YOU PUT ALL THE CHIPS DOWN...*
...on triple sixes, you jerk...
SURE. IF I'D WON, IT'D BE A 150 TO 1 PAYOUT.
150 TO 1 ON 50,000 YEN IS 7,500,000 YEN*, YOU KNOW.
WE'RE NOW BROKE BECAUSE YOU ***DIDN'T*** WIN!!
SHH!
DON'T SHOUT!
CASINOS ARE THE GATHERING PLACE OF GENTLE-MEN.
GAAAAAH!
IT'S OVER...
IT ALL ENDED IN A SECOND...
SLUMP
ALL RIGHT, ALL RIGHT...
sigh

*About $100 and $500, respectively.

**About $70,000 USD.

Good grief...
I'LL GO GET YOU SOME COFFEE TO CHEER YOU UP.
It's free!
I DON'T WANT ANY!!
stride stride
つかつか
stride
つか
LET'S SEE...
HE'S UPSET, SO MAYBE I'LL GET HIM SOME NICE, SUGARY COCOA.
stride stride
つかつか
zhoop
ずい
OOF.
THAT RICH SINGA-POREAN JERK...
...CUTTING IN LINE JUST BECAUSE I CAN'T SPEAK ENGLISH...
beep
ピッ
WHAM
ドン
HEY!
ポロ
PLOP

HUH?

SOME RICH GUY JUST DROPPED A 10,000 YEN CHIP?!

FOR REAL?

YES.

THANKS TO MY NIMBLE FOOT-WORK, HE DIDN'T NOTICE A THING.

I GOT IT IN A GENTLE-MANLY WAY.

SO.

THIS IS OUR FINAL PLAY.

SHALL WE GO...

...KURANO-SUKE-SAN?

Kid's Club
squeal
squeal
THEY'RE TAKING A WHILE...
I'M WORRIED...
HEY!
BIG SIS!
CAN YOU DRAW?
HUH?
OH, PICTURES?
D-DO YOU WANT ME TO DRAW ONE?
....
I...
I CAN ONLY DRAW SEA CREATURES, LIKE CLARA...
CLA...?
...RA?
UM...
IT'S "JELLY-FISH"...
...IN ENGLISH.
OH!!
JELLYFISH!!

skritch skritch skritch skritch skritch skritch
かきかき かきかき かきかき
ALL DONE!
WOW!
IT'S SOOOO GROSS!
OH, GOOD...
THEY LIKE IT...
ほっ
Phew!
OKAY, LOOK!
HERE'S A FLOWER HAT JELLY, AND THIS ONE IS A NOMURA'S JELLYFISH!
swip swip swip swip
WOW!
THEY'RE ALL CREEPY!
DRAW FLOWERS OR SOME-THING!
THIS GIRL IS WEIRD.
*Third time he's made this face today.
NO, NO, NO.
I'M GONNA HANDLE THIS ONE...
blaze
blaze
clench
DA-DUN

HAND IT OVER!
OH!
Yah!
DON'T YOU THINK YOU SHOULD BET ON MY LUCK?
LIKE HELL!
Your luck is non-existent!!
OKAY!
I'M HEADING TO THAT CROWDED TABLE.
clamor
clamor
YOU DON'T WANT TO GO BACK TO THAT BEAUTY?
NO, HER TABLE'S NO GOOD.
THERE WAS NO ONE THERE, REMEMBER?
WHAT I'M AFTER IS THE SWARM OF RICH GUYS...
THE TABLE WHERE THE BIG MONEY IS MOVING.

I WANT THE TABLE WITH THE HIGH-ROLLING BILLIONAIRES.
THE ONE WHERE ALL THE NUMBERS ARE COVERED IN CHIPS.
1-18
BECAUSE IF I WERE THAT TABLE'S DEALER...
...I'D BE EGGING THEM ON, GETTING THEM TO BET AND BET...
...AND THEN TAKING IT ALL AT THE BEST POSSIBLE MOMENT.
SO TODAY I'M GOING TO FOIL THE DEALER'S PLAN...
...AND USE THAT MOMENT TO MAKE OFF WITH THEIR POCKET CHANGE.
YOU SURE FIGURED THIS OUT IN A SHORT TIME...
YOU REALLY *ARE* SMART.
Wow...
THERE!
THAT TABLE!

SHOVE
EXCUSE ME, SORRY.
COMING THROUGH.
SHOVE
squeeze squeeze
thump
clink
Sio BO
Dica Tot
346 13
136 10
443 11
123 6
555 15
346 13
124 7
Wow!
NOT YET...
NOT YET...
clink
Woo-hoo!
Wow!
clink
GOTTA WAIT...
BET!
bam bam bam
NOW!
FWIP

chak
shoop
FINISH!
fwup
カラカラカラカラ
rattle rattle rattle rattle
clink
fwup

*Both about $15,000 USD.

THAT CHIP MADE US **17,000 SINGAPORE DOLLARS!***

THAT'S 1,500,000 JAPANESE YEN!*

THAT'S THANKS TO ME, YOU KNOW. I PICKED UP THE CHIP, YOU KNOW!

YOU'LL GIVE ME SOME, RIGHT?

YEAH, YEAH, IT'S THANKS TO YOUR FOOTWORK AND YOUR PLEBIAN HABIT OF PICKING UP SMALL CHANGE.

SO HOW SHALL WE SPLIT IT, KURA-NOSUKE-SAN?

ME 60%, YOU 40%?

WHY SHOULD YOU GET MORE THAN ME?!

SORRY, BUT I KNOW HOW I WANT TO SPEND THIS.
SINCE WE'VE ALREADY COME ALL THE WAY TO SINGAPORE...
smirk
...THERE'S NO HARM IN HAVING A LITTLE FUN!
PREDA
WH...
WHERE ARE WE GOING...
...DRESSED LIKE THIS?
I-It's too revealing...
OKAY, NOW WE'RE ALL IN DISGUISE!
YEEK!
WH-WHAT'S WITH THOSE OUTFITS?!
SWOOP

WE'LL KEEP IT LOW-PROFILE SO KAI DOESN'T FIND US. BUT BEFORE WE GO HOME, LET'S HAVE A NIGHT ON THE TOWN!

Now,
then.
Time to put a dress on the poor princess who was locked in the tower...
BAM

...and give her one good night of partying.
VROOM
WE'RE GONNA GO ALL OUT!
ALL OUT, I TELL YA!
MAYBE WE SHOULD SPEND IT ALL, THEN.
Mean-while ...
I-I GUESS...
...WE SHOULD START AT... A DEPART-MENT STORE...
DE-DE-DE...
DEPART-MENT STORE?!

Episode 0
On the Eve of Amars

トプン
bloop

Hello!
It's your favorite wandering marine product, Clara the spotted jelly!

As always, I've got nothing but free time!

Hey, they seem to have plenty of time on their hands, too!
The otaku are eating something together.

Oh!
I see they're having hotpot day again.
gobble gobble
ガ ガ

They really like hotpot.
They pretty much eat it all the time.
NWAAH!
NOTHING TASTES BETTER THAN OUR WEEKLY AMARS HOTPOT!

But I wonder...
Before they all lived at Amamizukan together...
尼
Nun

...what kinds of lives did they lead, exactly...?

Rewinding several years...

WHAT?
TURN OUR STUDENT BOARDING HOUSE INTO APART-MENTS?

MY REALTOR ADVISED ME TO!
YOU KNOW HOW THE AMAMIZU COLLEGE CAMPUS IS MOVING TO THE COUNTRY-SIDE.
YES ...
THAT MEANS THIS PLACE WILL EMPTY OUT...

BUT... WOULD ANYONE OTHER THAN A STUDENT REALLY WANT TO RENT IN SUCH A RUN-DOWN BOARDING HOUSE?

ペタッ
swip

Rooms for Rent
← Inquire Within
どすどす
clomp clomp
SIGH ... WHO KNOWS WHAT WILL HAPPEN NOW...

WELL! I'LL GO HAVE SOME TEA AND YOKAN.
ガチャ
ka-chak

じー
stare

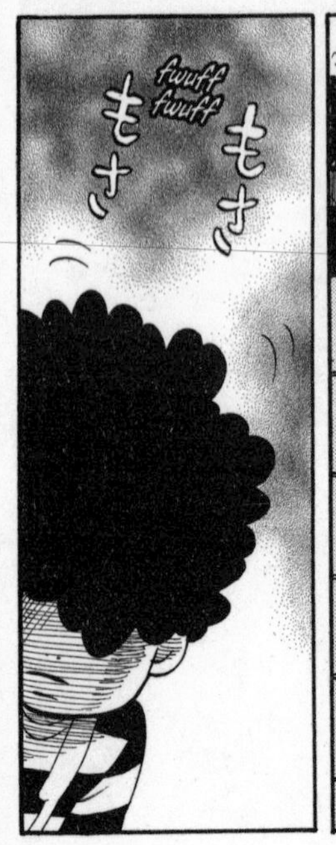
もさもさ
fwuff fwuff

shoop
Rooms for Rent
← Inquire Within
snap snap
LOOK WHAT I FOUND ON MY INSIDE-THE-YAMANOTE-LINE-ONLY TOKYO METRO ALL-STATION STOPOVER TRIP...
CHECK OUT THIS OLD-FASHIONED BUILDING...
APART-MENTS? NAH, A BOARDING HOUSE?

...
"ROOMS FOR RENT" ...
ka-chak
OH!
ARE YOU LOOKING FOR A ROOM?
flinch

PLEASE, FEEL FREE TO COME IN AND LOOK AROUND.
AS YOU CAN SEE, IT'S AN OLD BOARDING HOUSE, SO THE BATHROOMS ARE COMMUNAL, BUT THAT ALSO MEANS THE RENT IS LOW!
COM ...
mumble mumble
COM-MUNAL ...
RIGHT... I SEE...
YEAH ...
I'M... NOT SOMEONE WHO CAN HANDLE COMMUNAL LIVING.
WHAT?
swish

MAYA-CHAN!

MAYA-CHAN! HOW LONG ARE YOU GOING TO SLEEP ?!

I'M GOING TO WORK, OKAY?

WASH THE DISHES IN THE KITCHEN!

thump thump

HEY!

ARE YOU LISTENING TO ME?!

ANSWER ME, MAYA-CHAN!

thump thump thump

whirl
lurch
I CAN HEAR YOU JUST FINE! SHUT UP, WOMAN!!
The futon she's used since second grade.
OH, YOU!
HOW DARE YOU TALK TO YOUR MOTHER LIKE THAT?!
COME OUT HERE, YOU STUPID DAUGHTER!
THUMP THUMP
SHUT UP, SHUT UP, SHUT UP, SHUT UP!
ARGH!
I'LL MISS THE BUS!
FOR THE LOVE OF—
YOU WASH THE DISHES, GOT IT?!
huff huff
I TOLD YOU, I HEARD YOU!
SCRAM AL-READY!
SHEEESH!!
grrr
TONIGHT I'LL MAKE HER FATHER FINALLY LAY DOWN THE LAW!

tmp
tmp
tmp
トトト
shoop
ぬっ
pok
カパ
pat pat
ペタペタ
ぐるぐる
swirl
swirl
munch
munch
パクパク
nom
nom
もぐもぐ
sip sip
ズズ…

I'M GETTING OUT OF THIS STUPID HOUSE SOMEDAY ...!!
She says while eating breakfast her mother made.
DING-DONG
NWAH?!
WHO CALLS AT THIS EARLY HOUR?
It is 11 AM.
AH!
MAMI!
glow
tmp tmp tmp tmp
KA-CHAK
MAMI! IT'S BEEN A WHILE!
SORRY FOR COMING SO SUDDENLY, MAYA-CHAN.
NON-SENSE!
COME RIGHT IN! I SHALL MAKE US CHINESE TEA!!
MY NEW BOOK, THE ONE I WAS TELLING YOU ABOUT, CAME BACK FROM THE PRINTER YESTERDAY.
I REALLY WANT YOU TO BE THE FIRST ONE TO SEE IT...

THIS TIME I USED THE BATTLE OF CHANGBAN FOR MY SETTING.

NWAAAAHH!

蒼天已
黄天當立
歳在甲子
天下大吉

GUAN YU SHINES EVEN MORE IN THIS COMIC THAN HE DID IN YOUR LAST ONE!

I TRIED CHANGING MY ART STYLE A BIT.

LEAVE IT TO YOU, MAMI... I MEAN, ***WING SEKI-SENSEI.***

TO THINK I HAVE SUCH A FINE MANGA AUTHOR FOR A ***COUSIN!***

THOUGH I AM POOR, YOU ARE THE ONE THING I MAY TAKE PRIDE IN!!

tremble tremble

...should always be on me.

Wait!

Your eyes...

HEH, HEH... YOU'RE SO SILLY, MAYA-CHAN.

THE FIRST TIME I GAVE YOU MITSUTERU YOKOYAMA'S *THREE KINGDOMS* TO READ...

...YOU WERE ONLY A BABY.

YES, I REMEMBER IT WELL.

AND THE FIRST TIME I TOOK YOU TO A THREE KINGDOMS-ONLY EVENT...

I WAS IN FIRST GRADE!!

I KNOW, LET'S WATCH A DVD.

I RECORDED THE *GRAVES OF THE THREE KINGDOMS GENERALS* SHOW THAT AIRED ON BS THE OTHER DAY.

OH, THAT'S WON-DERFUL! I DON'T GET BS AT MY PLACE.

squeal squeal

I'm hooome!

BAM
HEY!
YOU HAVEN'T WASHED ANY DISHES!
nibble nibble
むっしゃむっしゃ
THAT'S BECAUSE MAMI CAME OVER...
WHAT? WHAT IS THIS?! YOU ORDERED OUT?! FOR SUSHI?!
DID MAMI-CHAN TREAT YOU?!
...
NO...
MAMI DOESN'T HAVE MONEY NOW, WITH COMIKET COMING UP...
I CAN'T BE-LIEVE YOU !!
YOU GOT GRANDPA TO PAY AGAIN, DIDN'T YOU?!
daze
YOU CAN'T KEEP TAKING ADVAN-TAGE OF HIM LIKE THAT JUST BECAUSE HE'S... HE'S LIKE THAT!
MAYA-CHAN! DO YOU REALIZE HOW MANY YEARS AGO YOU GRADUATED FROM HIGH SCHOOL?
PLEASE... I DON'T CARE IF IT'S PART TIME OR WHAT!
JUST GET A JOB!
I REFUSE !!

hush
ガチャ
ka-chak
I'M HOME.
I...
...AM GRACIOUSLY USING THE PENSION MONEY THAT GRANDPA HAS NO USE FOR!
YOU HAVE NO RIGHT TO SCOLD ME! I SHOULD BE THANKED!
WHAT?!
daze
I DO THE CHORES HERE, TOO.
THE ONLY "CHORE" YOU DO AROUND HERE IS CLEANING THE TUB.
AND YOU DON'T EVEN USE ACTUAL CLEANER—ALL YOU EVER DO IS GIVE IT A QUICK RINSE WITH WATER!
zwssh
sigh
YOU DON'T COOK, YOU DON'T DO LAUNDRY... YOU JUST LIE AROUND THE HOUSE EVERY DAY READING MANGA...
...
sigh
YOU'RE A GROWN WOMAN WHO HAS NO BOY-FRIEND, NO HUSBAND...
DON'T YOU FEEL ANY SHAME ABOUT YOUR LIFE-STYLE?!
DA-DUN
I FEEL NO SHAME!!

WELL, I...

...YOUR FATHER AND I...

...ARE ASHAMED FOR OUR NEIGHBORS TO SEE YOU!

Waah! わあっ

lurch

I AM NOT ASHAMED!!

THE EMOTION OF ***SHAME*** CAN BE EASILY OVERCOME THROUGH MENTAL TRAINING!!

IT IS NOT MY FAULT THAT I HAVE NO JOB.

OUR ERA IS AT FAULT!

mumble mumble もごもご

huff huff ハァ ハァ

I ... RAISED YOU WRONG...

MAYA-CHAN.

WHAT YOU NEED RIGHT NOW IS INDEPENDENCE.

Sign: White Rose Café

チラッ glance

chak カチャ…

ba-dum
トクン

clatter
カラ、コロ、

純喫茶
白ばら

I'M HOME ...

GAH!

SIS, YOU'RE HOME ALREADY?

びくっ flinch

SORRY ...

UM ...

...

AW, JEEZ!

I WAS ABOUT TO WATCH A DVD WITH MY FRIENDS!

sigh

DAISUKE-KUN ...

WH-WHAT ABOUT SCHOOL?

MIDTERMS ENDED TODAY, SO WE GOT TO GO HOME EARLY.

SIS, PLEASE!

GO SOMEWHERE FOR A LITTLE WHILE!

HUH?

fwip

A CAFÉ OR WHATEVER. YOU'VE GOT PLENTY OF PLACES TO GO, RIGHT?

PLEASE! GO KILL JUST TWO HOURS SOMEWHERE!

shove

OH ... OK ...

SAY...
HOW OLD IS YOUR BIG SISTER?
WHY'S SHE HOME IN THE AFTER-NOON?
gulp
ぎくっ
OH, RIGHT. SHE'S A NEET.
WHOA.
FOR REAL?
THEN SHE'S DOOMED.
Pfft!
プッ
Ha ha ha!
YEP, TOTALLY DOOMED!
Ah ha ha ha ha ha ha ha!
HERE WE GO.
AH.

daze
Oh!
OH, NO...!
lurch
ISAO HASHIZUME'S TUESDAY SUSPENSE THEATER IS RERUNNING AT 3:00...
...BUT I FORGOT TO SET A RECORD-ING!
tmp tmp tmp
jangle
DAI-SUKE-KUN!
SORRY, BUT I NEED TO SCHEDULE A—
CALL ME EMILY.
LET'S HAVE SOME FUN.

GOODNESS!
A MANGA AUTHOR?
THAT'S RIGHT. SHE CALLED YESTERDAY TO ASK ABOUT MOVING IN.
HAVE YOU HEARD OF JUON MEJIRO-SENSEI? IS SHE FAMOUS?
I DON'T KNOW... I ONLY READ WAKI YAMATO-SENSEI...
Like Asaki Yumemishi...
BUT... AREN'T A LOT OF MANGA ARTISTS...
...QUITE STRANGE?
WHAT?!
REALLY? MANGA ARTISTS ARE STRANGE?!
BUT THERE ARE PLENTY OF GREAT ONES, LIKE THE AUTHOR OF NORAKURO!
THAT'S NOT EVEN FROM THIS ERA!
That manga came out during the war!
THESE DAYS, ALL THE MANGA ARTISTS ARE...YOU KNOW...
I SUPPOSE YOU COULD SAY PERVERTS... OR MAYBE FAILURES AS PEOPLE...
REALLY?!
THEY'RE PERVERTS?!
OH NO, HOW SCARY!!

BUT, BUT, SHE SAID SHE'D PAY THE WHOLE FIRST YEAR'S RENT IN ADVANCE, SO...
WHAT?
DON'T TELL ME YOU ALREADY MADE THE DEAL?!
YEAH...
OH, MOTHER, YOU JUST NEVER LEARN!
SIGH
WHAT WILL WE DO IF A CRAZY PERVERT COMES?!
I'M SO WOR-RIED!
ガラ
rattle
ガラ
rattle
ガラ
rattle

chirp chirp

チュンチュン

WHAT?

THE MANGA ARTIST HAS ALREADY MOVED IN?!

YES, THIS MORNING AT 6:00...

HER ONLY LUGGAGE WAS A TRUNK AND A DUFFLE BAG...

WHAT WAS SHE LIKE?!

HOW OLD?! FAT? THIN?

WELL...

HER EYES WERE COVERED BY THIS...ARE THEY CALLED HEADSCARVES? YOU KNOW, THOSE PROTECTIVE HEAD COVERINGS THAT BOXERS WEAR...

A HOOD? DO YOU MEAN A HOOD?!

RIGHT, A HOOD!

I COULDN'T REALLY TELL BECAUSE OF HER HOOD!

HONESTLY!

MOTHER, YOU ARE JUST SO...

ピンポーン

DING-DONG

HEAVENS!

AN-OTHER VISITOR...

ka-chak

ガチャ

BRO...

BROC-COLI...

WH-WHO IS THIS?

WHAT DO THEY HAVE ON THEIR HEAD?!

ピンポーン

DING-DONG

U-
UM...
I...SAW THE SIGN OUTSIDE ABOUT ROOMS ...
OH, MY!
TWO JUST CAME IN AT ONCE...
LOOM
skreeee
TMP
TMP
TMP
HUH ?!
ZSH
huff
huff
huff
crying
SAW... SAW... SAW...
SAW?
I SAW THE SIGN FOR ROOMS!
ROOMS ROOMS ROOMS FOR RENT...
I SAW THE SIGN!
I AM A HUMBLE COMMONER DESIROUS OF A ROOM!!
Th-This person is strange in so many ways!

HERE ARE THE ROOMS FOR RENT.

EACH APARTMENT HAS A 6-TATAMI ROOM AND A 3-TATAMI ONE.

THE WINDOWS ARE EQUIPPED WITH LAUNDRY-DRYING POLES—

troop troop

SHFF

EEP!

twitch

WHAT?!

A PAPER JUST SLID OUT FROM UNDER THE DOOR...

IT'S A GHOST!

A GHOST!

ACK!

THE GHOST!

SORRY...

THE GHOST APOLOGIZED!!

I'm alive...

MM.

SOMETHING'S WRITTEN HERE...

NO, STOP, IT'S TOO SCARY!

Yeek!

HUH?!

turn

ANYBODY HERE GOT NIMBLE FINGERS?

FLUMP
FLUMP
skritch skritch skritch
rub rub
Heh heh...
IT LOOKS LIKE THINGS HAVE GOTTEN ROUGH!
MY GOODNESS...
OKAY... THIS ONE'S DONE...
BLACK IN THE HAIR ON THIS PAGE, PLEASE.
THE SO-CALLED "SPOT BLACKS," EH?
I HAVE A CHARISMATIC DOUJINSHI ARTIST FOR A COUSIN, SO I HAVE EXPERIENCE IN MOST OF THESE TASKS ...
IF YOU SEE ANYTHING TRICKY, LEAVE IT TO ME!
OH... PLEASE HELP WITH THIS, THEN.
NWAH!
WHAT IS THIS?! GUO JIA MAY BE CAPABLE OF SUCH INSUFFERABLY COMPLEX PROCESSES, BUT I AM NOT.
MM?
GINZA LINE, EH?
I CAN DRAW THIS WITHOUT A REF-ERENCE PHOTO.
shff
WHAT ?!

IN THAT CASE...
...I'LL DO THE SALT-AND-PEPPER HAIR FOR THIS MAN WHO MUST BE THE MAIN CHARACTER'S FATHER.
Heh heh...
I SEE YOU ALL HAVE CLEARLY-DEFINED SPECIALTIES...
IN THAT CASE, I'LL DRAW THE FLAG OF WEI HERE!
ALL THOSE WHO SEE WEI AS UNIFIER, GATHER UNDER WEI'S BANNER!
FWOOP
NO, YOU CAN'T ADD IN THINGS ON YOUR OWN.
IN THAT CASE, I'LL DRAW THE NOZOMI N700 HERE!
...
snatch
WHAT ?!
WHA...
WHAT IS THIS...?
TWO...
TWO MEN...
...ARE KISSING EACH OTHER!
YES...
YOU SHOULDN'T LOOK, MOTHER...
WHY AREN'T ANY OF YOU SHOCKED BY THIS?!
OH...
WELL, IT'S LIKE...
THIS IS PRETTY MUCH **BASIC KNOWL-EDGE** STUFF FOR US...
Hello!
Motorcycle express courier here!

THANKS A MILLION. I'LL ASK AGAIN NEXT TIME.

shump

simmer simmer

WELCOME TO AMAMIZUKAN, EVERYONE!
AND HERE'S TO OUR SUDDEN HARD WORK!
CHEERS!!

*About $100 USD.

LOOK HOW MUCH MEAT I BOUGHT WITH MEJIRO-SENSEI'S 10,000 YEN!*
WOO!
MEAT!
Let's chow dooo-own!
gobble gobble
munch munch
NGH!
OH NO!
WHAT'S WRONG?! ARE YOU CHOK-ING?!

UNGH...
UNGH-NGH....
plip
I-I APOLOGIZE...
IT'S JUST... I WAS ASKING MYSELF...
...HOW LONG IT'S BEEN SINCE I HAD SUCH A FUN...
...MEAL...
UNGH!
scrub
E-EVERYONE...
ngh sniff ngh...
SKRUT
I MAY NOT BE WORTHY, BUT...
...I LOOK FORWARD TO LIVING TOGETHER.
sniff sniff
deep bow
skrut
NO, NO...
WE FEEL THE SAME...
UM, BY THE WAY...
ISN'T THE MANGA ARTIST DINING WITH US?
I INVITED HER, BUT APPARENTLY SHE DOESN'T LIKE TO BE SEEN BY PEOPLE.
klat

shff
スッ
ME-JIRO-SEN-SEI.
I MADE SUKIYAKI WITH THE MONEY YOU GAVE US, SO I'M LEAVING SOME HERE FOR YOU...
twitch
ぴくっ
ka-chak
ガチャ
SWIVEL
SLAM
バタン
...
SAY, CHIEKO-CHAN...
I KNOW IT'S A BIT LATE TO BE ASKING THIS, BUT...
THOSE TENANTS ARE ALL...
... WOMEN ...
RIGHT ??

I... I THINK SO...
Although some of them are ambiguous...
IN THAT CASE...
SINCE WE'VE JUST ACQUIRED SO MANY FEMALE TENANTS AT ONCE...
...IT'S PROBABLY BEST TO JUST DECLARE THIS BOARDING HOUSE WOMEN-ONLY.
WE WOULDN'T WANT A MALE TENANT TO COME ALONG AND CAUSE MISTAKES TO BE MADE.
I DON'T THINK "MISTAKES" ARE LIKELY, BUT YES.
THAT DOES SEEM BEST.

Well, anyway...

A lot happened, but I think these folks must've found their place to belong.

Not that *I* can criticize!

After all, I spend every day floating around here.

Amamizukan is a really comfortable place.

It's just like the ocean.

天水館

Circled: 9.55 "A Stroll for the Middle-Aged"
Tsuruo Karasawa goes on a gem of a path!

キュッ SQUEAK

キュッ SQUEAK

キュッ SQUEAK

キュッ SQUEAK

Circled: 10.15 Suspense "The Steam Murder" (Rerun). 10.30 "The Spoiled Shogun" Ken Sugihara, Jun Yoshimura, Yoko Hoshino, and others.

Special Interview

We Snuck Behind the Scen

パラ… flip

Whew...

カチ click

パラ
flip
POPULAR YOUNG ACTOR SATORU KAKUTA!!
Inter-view About the Newest TV Drama

hush
Jiji-sama's Moe Meter

パラ
flip
SCHOOL OF HOTTIES
Huge Behind-the Scenes Special!

hush

パラ
flip
パラ
flip
新ドラマインタビュー
徹底解剖!

パラ
flip
Inter-view with School Principal Kiyoshi Kobe

パラ…
flip

キュゥゥーー!
FWEEEE...

パラ
flip
Silver Anniversary Trip
Together for a lifetime.

!!!
ギリュイイイイーー
SQUEEEEEEEE

CRACK

THIS IS DEFINITELY THE ONE WE WANT TO WATCH!
MUST-SEE DVD CORNER
YUTAKA MIZUTANI
YASUFUMI TERAWAKI
相棒
season 5
Aibou Season 5 • DVDBOX

WHAT?
YOU NEED TO RECORD THIS MANY SHOWS AGAIN?
SORRY... THIS WEEK THERE ARE RERUNS OF ISAO HASHI-ZUME'S *KYOTO MEIKYU ANNAI*...
...AND RERUNS OF AIBOU, SO...
LET'S SEE, HERE'S THE GUIDE...AND I'LL RECORD FROM THE LIST... *AIBOU, AIBOU, AIBOU...*
Ah, found it.
SORRY ...
IF I HAD MONEY, I'D BUY THE DVD BOX...
...BUT IT'S TOO MUCH FOR SOMEONE LIVING ON AN ALLOW-ANCE...
THUMP THUMP THUMP

Princess Jellyfish Heroes - Part 11/End

キュゥゥー!
FWEEEE

Extra Episode
Princess Jellyfish
Bonus Manga

Thank you for buying Volume 8, everyone. I'm Akiko Higashimura.

Princess Jellyfish recently got adapted into a movie, so I've been doing interviews and such, appearing in front of people quite a bit.
I'm 39, yet I'm dressed like this...
Each month is so hectic, I don't have time for day-dreaming.

If you're wondering about my Amars activities lately...
Oh, right, I told you in Volume 7 that I'm hooked on camping... but there've been so many typhoons that I can hardly go.
ZWSSSH
This week is a no-go!

So whenever I get a moment's free time these days...
...I just lie down on the sofa. That's all.
motionless

じ motionless ....

Emotionally Numb

When I lie still like that, my otaku husband tries to show me his anime recordings, so...

shff スッ

PUT IN THE DVD OF THAT FOREIGN DRAMA I RENTED!

NO!

...

Damn.

And whenever I'm watching foreign dramas...

...Gocchan is bound to finish his homework and come ask me...

HEY, MAMA.

FOR BREAKFAST TOMORROW...

ガチャ ka-chak

...HOW ABOUT WE HAVE OSHIRUKO?

SHEESH, AGAIN?

キリッ shing

That's right, Gocchan loves red beans, and he takes advantage of any opening he has to plot ways to eat *ohagi* or *oshiruko*.

He 100% inherited this from me.

When I was a kid, I really, really loved red bean paste. I've been told that once, when I was invited to my relatives' place around age three or four, there was an incident where I ate the fillings out of every single *manju* they had.

Apparently, I only ate the bean paste.

Yep, when Koike-san from Toyokuni Printing came to my office a while back...

Hello.
loom

...bearing super-delicious *taiyaki* from Naniwaya, one of my favorite shops...

GOCCHAN! SOMEONE GAVE US *TAIYAKI*!

I didn't have that many assistants today, so there were three left over!

WHAT?!

LET'S MAKE THEM TOMORROW'S BREAKFAST, THEN.

NICE!

shing

WHY ARE YOU TRYING TO ESTABLISH RED BEAN PASTE AS A MORNING FOOD?!

And the other day when we went to a department store on an errand...

I HAVE AN IDEA! LET'S BUY SOMETHING AT THE DELI DOWNSTAIRS!

NICE.

WOW.
THEY ALL LOOK SO GOOD, I CAN'T DECIDE.
WHAT ARE YOU HUNGRY FOR, GOCCHAN?
MEAT? FISH?
SHOOP
HMM? GOCCH—
HUH?!
WHY ARE YOU IN THAT LINE?

OH!

staaare

TOKACHI OHAGI

WAIT... UH, GOCCHAN, DID YOU WANT *OHAGI*?

HMM... SORTA KINDA?

Always projects an "I don't like them much" attitude.

OKAY, FINE.
HERE, BUY SOME WITH THIS.
MAMA DOESN'T WANT ANY, SO JUST BUY ENOUGH FOR YOU.
About two?
500 Yen
AH!
THANKS, MAMA.
SIX OHAGI, PLEASE.
shff
YOU'RE BUYING SIX?!
HOLD IT. TWO IS ENOUGH, OKAY? MAMA AND PAPA ARE ON A DIET, SO WE WON'T EAT ANY.
NO PROBLEM. IF THERE ARE LEFT-OVERS, I'LL HAVE THEM FOR BREAKFAST TOMORROW.
shing

So yeah...
...we're living a fun life!
Still, 2014 was a chaotic year due to the Princess Jellyfish movie.
Amars and Kura-pyon are all really, really great in this movie, so please watch it!
Just go watch ota-cute Rena Nōnen!!

THIS MANGA'S GONNA BE A MOVIE ...?!
Eeeeeee
REALLY ?! FOR REALS ?!
SHOCK!!!
SO WHO WILL BE PLAY-ING THE STAR, ME, CLARA?!
HUH? WHO'S THIS? NEVER HEARD OF HER!
A ROOKIE ?! WHO'S HER MAN-AGER?
I DON'T KNOW ABOUT THIS!

HM?
YOU WANT TO SEE *ME* TRY ON NEW OUT OUTFITS, TOO?
OOH!
TODAY'S FASHION THEME IS "MR. KURARA," RELIABLE REGULAR AT THE "KURAGE" LOCAL BAR!

EVERYONE!

THE PRINCESS JELLYFISH MOVIE! I CAN'T BELIEVE IT! IT'S AN IMPOSSIBLY FUN HEARTTHROBBING EXPLOSIVELY BEAUTIFUL MOVIE! MY HEART IS STILL BEATING SO FAST IT MIGHT BURST OUT OF MY CHEST!! I'M ON THE EDGE OF A MEDICAL EMERGENCY!! FWOOOOOOO!!

-AKIKO HIGASHIMURA

DEAR READERS! LATELY, I'VE GOTTEN OBSESSED WITH SO MANY THINGS, IT'S BECOMING A PROBLEM! I THOUGHT THAT WHEN I BECAME AN ADULT, I'D GRADUALLY CALM DOWN, BUT IT'S ONLY GETTING WORSE AND WORSE. PLEASE SAVE ME!

-AKIKO HIGASHIMURA

Episode 78
Singapore@DEEP

The act of buying clothes...
NISETAN
ドーン
DA-DUN

SO.
WHY DO I GOTTA COME ON YER SHOPPIN' TRIP?
I wore normal clothes insteada my sari so I'd fit in, but still.
B-BE-CAUSE...
...WE CAN'T ENTER A DEPART-MENT STORE WITHOUT BACKUP...
CORRECT! WE FEEL UNEASY ALONE! PLEASE COME WITH US!
YER FINE. YA BROUGHT A TON OF MONEY TO SHOP HERE, SO TO THE STORE, YER VALUABLE CUSTOMERS.
HOLD YER HEADS HIGH!

YA GOT THE RIGHT APPROACH, THOUGH.
IT'S GOOD FOR PEOPLE WHO WANNA SELL CLOTHES TO TRY BUYIN' SOME WITH THEIR OWN MONEY.
I SEE YA FINALLY DEVELOPED ENOUGH TO THINK ABOUT THAT.

IN HUMAN TERMS, YA MADE IT TO AGE 13!
YER SICK OF THE CLOTHES YER PARENTS GOT YA, SO YER GOIN' OUT TO BUY YER OWN WITH YER NEW YEAR'S CASH. EXACTLY LIKE 13-YEAR-OLDS!
"IN HUMAN TERMS"?! WE ARE HUMAN, MADAM!
LOOK...
MAGGOTS ARE EATING IN HERDS...
Café
Ah ha ha! That's so weird!
Right?!
AHA, THOSE MUST BE WHAT PEOPLE CALL "SWEETS-BRAINED GIRLS"...*

*A term for a girl who mindlessly follows trends.

SPARKLE
SPARKLE
キラキラー
OKAY, SHUT UP. DON'T TALK. YA EMBARRASS ME WHEN YA TALK.
NOW LET'S GO.
NISHA-SAN, I'LL JUST GO TO WHERE THE KIMONO ARE ON THE 7TH FLOOR...
NOPE! No runnin' away!

HELLO!
WE'RE HERE TO SEE YER LINEUP.
ピキィ
KRIKT
ズカズカ
stride
stride

WEL-COME!
THANKS.
YA CAN JUST PICK OUT SOME STUFF FOR THOSE GIRLS.
THEY'VE NEVER BOUGHT ANY NICE CLOTHES THEM-SELVES.
WHAT?!
WHY MUST YOU ABRUPTLY BETRAY OUR SECRETS?!
カァァァ blush
TRAITOR!

OH, I SEE!
I LOOK FORWARD TO THE CHAL-LENGE.
Get over here.
COME ON! IT'S OKAY, THIS LADY'S NICE.
shff
ス
flinch
ビクッ
カチャカチャ
shak shak
SALE
WEL-COME!
サッ
fwoop
じー…
staaare
HERE.
THIS ONE, PLEASE.
THANK YOU VERY MUCH!
THESE ARE SO SIMPLE AND CON-VENIENT.
I HAVE TWO MYSELF!
A GRAY ONE AND A NAVY ONE!
I'M FEELING CHILLY TODAY...
OH, I KNOW, THE TEMPERATURE FELL SO SUDDENLY! IT'S THE SORT OF WEATHER THAT MAKES US ALL WANT ANOTHER LAYER, ISN'T IT?
WELL, I DEFINITELY RECOMMEND THIS, ESPECIALLY SINCE IT'S ON SALE!
ゴクッ
gulp

NOW, THEN! WHAT KIND OF THING ARE YOU LOOKING FOR?

EEK!

shoop

W-WAIT... STRANGERS SHOULDN'T ASK YOSUI INOUE-TYPE QUESTIONS LIKE THAT.*

WHAT IS YOUR INTENT? ARE YOU SEEKING A CONCRETE ANSWER, LIKE "PANTS" OR "CULOTTES"? WELL, WENCH?!

HEY!!

QUIT BEIN' RUDE, YA IDIOTS!

AND QUIT TALKIN' TO DOLLS!

Do you want me to make you a new outfit, honey?

I'm having chest pains!

*A Japanese songwriter known for his surreal lyrics.

NO, NO, OF COURSE NOT. IF YOU COULD JUST GIVE ME A ROUGH IMAGE OF WHAT YOU'RE LOOKING FOR...
FOR EXAMPLE, WHETHER YOU WANT CLOTHES FOR PARTIES, OR WORK, OR DATES...
THIS CROWD DON'T GO TO PARTIES OR WORK OR DATES, BUT THEY SAY THEY WANNA TRY BUYIN' CLOTHES.
AS PEOPLE.
STOP SPEAKING OF US LIKE WE'RE LESS THAN HUMAN!
OH, OKAY... SO... THEY'RE LOOKING FOR CASUAL CLOTHES, RIGHT?
IF YA GOTTA CLASSIFY IT, THEY WANT CLOTHES TO WEAR WHEN THEY'RE BUYIN' CLOTHES. *Basically.*
HOW ABOUT THIS SUIT SET, THEN?
IT JUST CAME IN TODAY!
THE CUT IS VERY SIMPLE, SO ANYONE CAN PULL IT OFF.
NOT BAD.
"SUIT SET"?
LIKE THE SETS IN VOLLEY-BALL?
HEY, JIJI.
TRY THIS ON!
HUH?
AH!
O-OKAY...
swivel
T-TRY IT ON...?!
HEY, BE CAREFUL! DON'T THEY MAKE YOU BUY IT IF YOU PUT IN ON?
JIJI-SAMA, YOU NEED TO CHECK THE PRICE FIRST.
OH!
RIGHT.
LET'S SEE...
mumble mumble

*About $360 USD.

*About $260 USD.

...
WHAT IS IT, JIJI?!
NISHA-SAN...
...I...
I CAN'T DECIDE.
WHAT?
I HAVE NO IDEA WHERE TO START...
...FIGURING OUT WHICH STORE TO PICK AND THEN WHICH CLOTHES TO PICK.
YA CAN JUST BUY WHATEVER GIVES YA INSPIRATION—MAKES YA THINK "THIS IS NICE."
YA GOT THE MONEY, RIGHT?
...
INSPIRATION...

SO... IF A PERSON HAS NO INSPIRATION...
...HOW SHOULD THEY CHOOSE WHAT CLOTHES TO BUY?
I MEAN, WHEN SOMETHING COSTS 30,000 YEN...*
...YOU HAVE TO HAVE A GOOD REASON TO BUY IT, RIGHT?

*About $300 USD.

MAYBE RICH PEOPLE ARE DIFFERENT.
BUT NORMAL PEOPLE WORK AS HARD AS THEY CAN...
...AND THEY USE THE PRECIOUS WAGES FROM THEIR JOBS TO BUY THESE CLOTHES...

HOW DO THEY ALL DECIDE, UNDER THOSE CONDITIONS?

ブオーン
VROOM
OKAY!
WE HAVE ALL NIGHT. WHERE SHOULD WE GO?
My wig's coming off!
I'M DYING OF HUNGER HERE, SO PLEASE FEED US FIRST.
NICE IDEA. I'M STARVING, TOO.
I VOTE CURRY IN LITTLE INDIA...
...OR DIM SUM AND PEKING DUCK IN CHINA-TOWN.
EATING SOME LAMB ON ARAB STREET SOUNDS GOOD, TOO.
UH-HUH...
YOU'RE VERY KNOWL-EDGEABLE, HANA-MORI-SAN...
YES.
I STUDIED THE *CO-TRIP* GUIDE-BOOK ON THE PLANE.
I'M THE TYPE WHO THOROUGHLY RESEARCHES HIS DESTINATION CITY BEFORE EVERY TRIP.
MMM, I CAN'T DECIDE. I WANNA EAT ALL OF THOSE.
DO YOU?
IN THAT CASE...

...LET'S GO SOMEPLACE WHERE YOU CAN EAT IT ALL.
chatter
clamor
chatter
wuzza
WHOA! IS THIS A MARKET?
A HAWKER CENTER. IN JAPANESE TERMS, I SUPPOSE IT'S A CLUSTER OF STREET STANDS, OR MAYBE A FOOD COURT?
THERE ARE STALLS HERE WITH ALL KINDS OF FOOD.
She put on....
...her glasses.
chatter clamor chatter clamor
WOW ...
Yay!
OKAY! I'M STARTING WITH CHICKEN CURRY!
I'M GOING FOR DUMPLINGS AND BROTH!
...
OH, WOW...
THE PEOPLE ARE ALL DRESSED DIFFER-ENTLY...

ガヤ
clamor
ガヤ
clamor
キャッ キャッ
chatter chatter
IT'S REALLY STRANGE.
PEOPLE IN ETHNIC CLOTHES FROM ALL SORTS OF COUNTRIES...
...ARE ALL LIVING IN THIS PLACE FULL OF SKY-SCRAPERS.
I RE-MEM-BER...
...THOSE WOMEN'S SCARVES.
I SAW ON TV THAT THEY WEAR THEM FOR RELIGIOUS REASONS.

They have a god they believe in...
...and it determines what clothes they wear.
There's a reason they're dressed like that.
I've never even thought about my reasons.
Something cheap.
And comfy.
And in a plain color, so I don't stand out.
Those are the only criteria I've ever used to pick my clothes.
And I doubt I even realized them.
HEY!
THIS LOOKED SO TASTY, I GOT SOME FOR YOU, TOO!
OH!
THANK YOU...
blink

MAYBE WE ORDERED TOO MUCH.
Ha ha ha!
WHAT'S THE HARM? WE HAVE PLENTY OF MONEY.
MM-HMM! THISH ISH GOOD!
OH. THIS CURRY HAS CHICKEN IN IT, HUH?
HMM? YEAH.
Yum.
I HAD FISH CURRY BEFORE...
...SO I THOUGHT MAYBE ALL CURRY HERE USED FISH.
INTER-ESTING. WAS IT GOOD?
OH, YES, VERY...
WHERE'D YOU EAT IT?
UM... "LITTLE INDIA," I THINK?
HUH?! WHO TOOK YOU *THERE?*
I know you couldn't get there by yourself.
HUH? OH. THE CEO.

...
WAS IT JUST THE TWO OF YOU?
UM, YES... HUH?!
IT WAS A DATE.
WHAT?!
THAT CEO IS INTO YOU, TSUKIMI-SAN.
HE WOULDN'T HAVE BROUGHT YOU ALL THE WAY HERE OTHERWISE.
WHAT A CREEP.
HE'S GOT A LOLITA COMPLEX!
SHEESH, I WANT TO LIVE IN SINGAPORE. I'D SLEEP WITH THE CEO MYSELF, IF IT GOT ME A POSITION AS HIS PERSONAL CHAUFFEUR.
...
HEY.
HE DIDN'T DO ANYTHING WEIRD TO YOU, DID HE?
HUH?!
N-N-N-NOTHING WEIRD, NO...
DA-DA-DUN
オオオオ
THAT WAS JUST A GREETING, SO...
SUSPICIOUS!
I BET HE AT LEAST HELD YOUR HAND, RIGHT?

AH!

NOW, THEN!
WE ATE PLENTY, SO LET'S HEAD TO A CLUB OR SOMETHING!

AVIDY.

HUH?
...LOOKS KIND OF EMPTY TO ME.
UGH! NOT THAT GIANT SIGN AGAIN!
THE STUPID THING IS EVERY-WHERE!
...
IT...

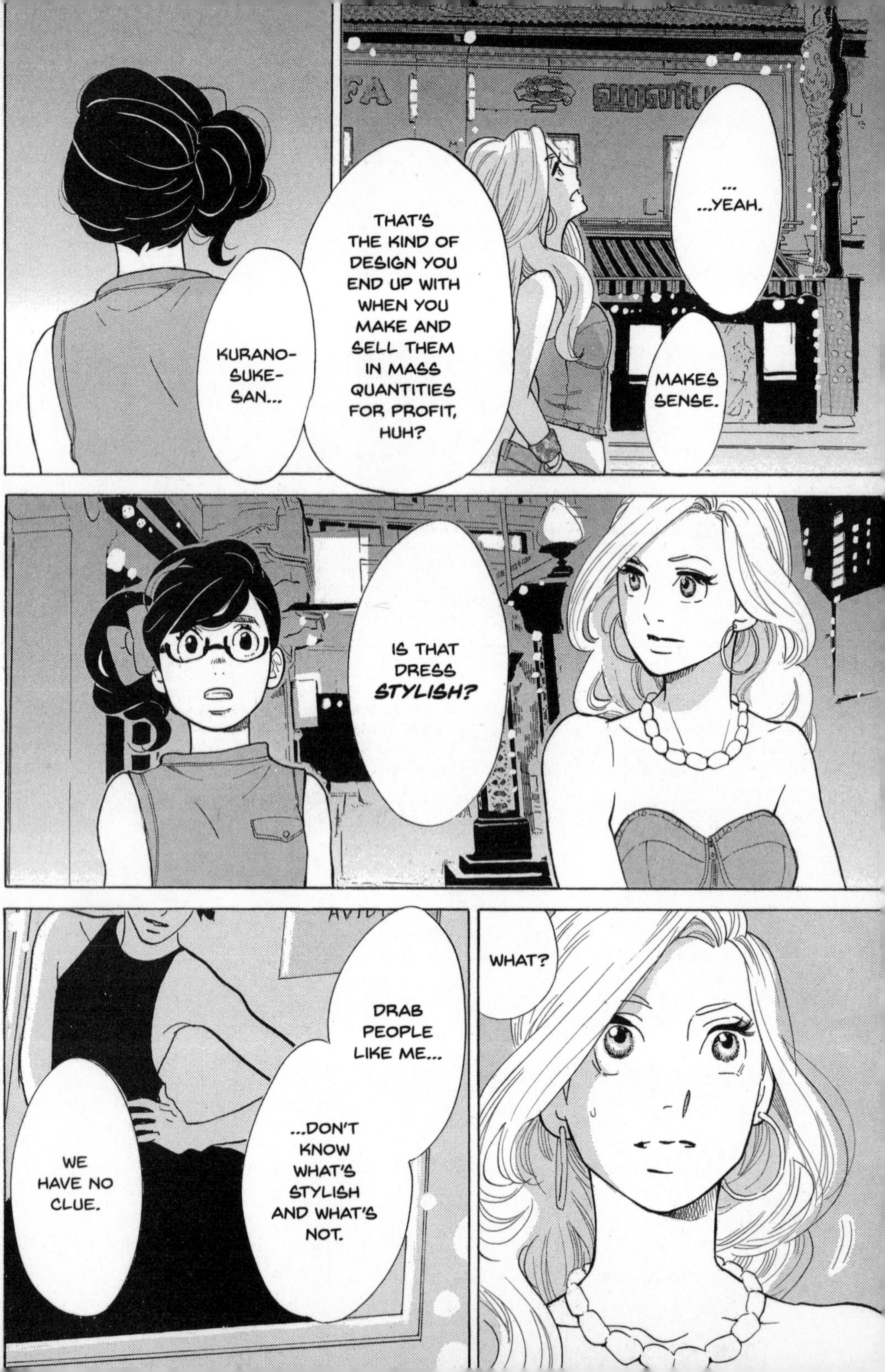

...
...YEAH.
MAKES SENSE.
THAT'S THE KIND OF DESIGN YOU END UP WITH WHEN YOU MAKE AND SELL THEM IN MASS QUANTITIES FOR PROFIT, HUH?
KURANO-SUKE-SAN...

BUT TO ME, THE PEOPLE AT THE HAWKER CENTER...
...WELL...
...THEY WEREN'T EMPTY, I GUESS?
TH-THEY WERE WEARING THOSE CLOTHES FOR A REASON...
...AND THAT'S REALLY ...
I-I'M NOT SURE HOW TO PUT IT...
...
TSUKIMI.
FINISHING THAT TRAIN OF THOUGHT IS OUR WHOLE JOB.

YOUR FEELINGS RIGHT NOW AS A DESIGNER...
...AND THE WORDS YOU'RE LOOKING FOR.
I'LL FIGURE THEM OUT...
...AND ARTICULATE THEM.
AND THAT'LL BECOME THE CONCEPT BEHIND THE JELLY FISH BRAND. I'M SURE OF IT.
THE CLOTHES WE MAKE ARE DIFFERENT THAN THE ONES THEY MAKE...

...AND I'M GONNA PROVE IT.
KURANO-SUKE-SAN...
trot trot
KURANO-SUKE-SAN!
CHECK IT OUT: I BOUGHT A BUDDHA.
YOU WHAT?
WHILE YOUR HUMBLE HANAMORI ADHERES TO NO RELIGION, WHEN YOU GET TO BE MY AGE, SOMETIMES WHEN YOU'RE ALONE AT NIGHT YOU THINK ABOUT YOUR RETIRE-MENT YEARS AND START TO PANIC. I THOUGHT LOOKING AT THIS BUDDHA FIGURE WOULD HELP ME GET TO SLEEP AT TIMES LIKE THAT.
I SUPPOSE I'M AT AN AGE WHERE I WANT A GOD ALL TO MYSELF.
EX-CUSE ME?!
HOW MUCH DID THAT COST?

HMM? IT WAS CHEAP. ABOUT 50,000 YEN.
I BOUGHT IT WITH THE CASINO MONEY.
WHAT?! YOU CAN GET ONE OF THOSE FOR 50,000 YEN?
HOW MANY DOLLARS WAS IT?
HMM? FIVE THOUSAND.
HUH?
YOU MEAN FIVE HUNDRED?
HMM?
WELL... NOW I'M NOT SURE ANYMORE.
BUT I PAID WITH FIVE BILLS THAT LOOKED LIKE 10,000 YEN BILLS, SO...
SAY WHAT?!
LURCH
HOLD ON, WERE THOSE THOUSAND-DOLLAR BILLS?!
GAAH, I KNEW IT!
SINGAPORE HAS THOUSAND-DOLLAR BILLS...
...AND EACH ONE'S WORTH ABOUT A *HUNDRED THOUSAND* YEN!
THEY SOLD YOU THAT BUDDHA FOR 500,000 YEN!
WHAT?!
AW, SHOOT.
That's expensive!
"SHOOT" DOESN'T COVER IT! GO RETURN THAT RIGHT NOW!
WELL, A MAN WAS SELLING IT ON THE STREET, SO...
OH, HE'S GONE.
ARE YOU KIDDING ME?!
WHAT'S WRONG WITH YOU, YOU IDIOT?!
LISTEN, YOUNG MAN, YOU MUSTN'T CALL YOUR ELDERS "IDIOTS"!
HANAMORI, YOU MORON! YOU STUPID *IDIOT!*

WAIT A SECOND! WE MADE ONE AND A HALF MILLION YEN AT THE CASINO, THEN BOUGHT THESE CLOTHES, AND THEN THERE'S OUR ROUND-TRIP FLIGHTS, AND TSUKIMI'S RETURN FLIGHT, AND...
OH! AND THE RENTAL CAR FEE...
IF YOU BOUGHT A 500,000 YEN BUDDHA ON TOP OF THAT, IT MEANS WE'RE TOTALLY BROKE AGAIN!!
WHOOPS.
SEE, THE ONE PART OF THE GUIDEBOOK I DIDN'T READ WAS THE "CURRENCY IN SINGAPORE" SECTION...

Book: Co-Trip

ゴ
VRRRR
オ

KURANO-SUKE-SAN, I KNOW I MADE A MISTAKE, SO WE CAN PUT THIS BUDDHA AT AMAMIZUKAN AND MAKE IT THE HOUSEHOLD GOD IF YOU WANT.

...

YOU DON'T MIND? EVERYONE WILL BE THRILLED.

REALLY?!

I'm sleepy.

THERE, SEE? NOW QUIT SULKING, KURANO-SUKE-SAN.

ROLLING WITH THE PUNCHES IS A KEY LIFE SKILL.

...

Even Buddha says so.

OH!
chant chant
ブツブツ
DEAR BUDDHA, PLEASE LET ME KISS A BEAUTIFUL WOMAN, TOO!
THAT'S A CRAPPY WISH!
SO PEOPLE IN SINGAPORE REALLY DO KISS AS A GREETING. I KNEW IT.
ほっ Phew!
HUH?
NO, THOSE ARE AMERICAN TOURISTS.
WHAT ?!
I'M PRETTY SURE PEOPLE DON'T KISS HELLO IN SINGA-PORE.
WH-WHAT ?!
MAYBE MR. FISH IS AMERICAN, THEN.
HIS LAST NAME IS ENGLISH, AFTER ALL...
WHAT?
WHAT'S WITH YOU?
ぴくっ twitch
DID THAT CEO KISS YOU HELLO?
WHERE?
ON THE CHEEK?
...
AH...
WELL... UM...

NO WAY...
ON THE MOUTH?!
!!
カァァァ
BLUSSSH
ブチ
SNAP
THAT JERK!
OH, I AM TAKING HIM DOWN!!

SIR.
I'M LEAVING THE COMPANY.
I'VE JUST FILLED OUT THE PAPERWORK.
I APOLOGIZE FOR RELEASING HER AGAINST YOUR ORDERS.
GOODBYE, SIR.

WHAT'LL YOU DO NOW?
GO SELL YOURSELF TO A RIVAL COMPANY...
...AND START DEALING BASED ON THIS ONE'S BUSINESS MODEL?
NO.
I'LL GO WAIT TABLES AT A CHINESE RESTAURANT SOMEWHERE.
I'M SICK OF THIS BUSINESS.

The reason we wear clothes...
...will become the reason we make clothes, too.
I'M HOME!
I, THE UNWORTHY TSUKIMI KURASHITA, AM ASHAMED TO SAY I MADE IT BACK ALIVE!

Episode 79
Amars' Feast

TSUKI-MIIIII!

Welcome home, Tsukimi!!

WE ARE SOOOOORRY!!

WE ARE TERRIBLE PEOPLE WHO PRACTICALLY SOLD YOU, OUR COMRADE, FOR MONEY!!
WOW, SUKI-YAKI!
THIS IS AMAZ-ING...!!
simmer
simmer

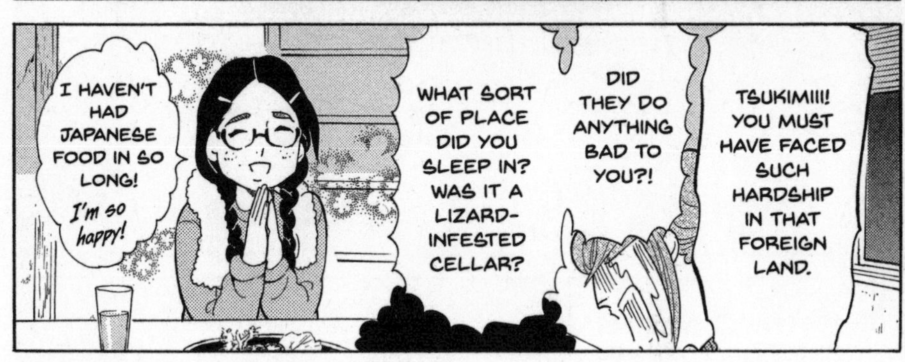
TSUKIMI!!! YOU MUST HAVE FACED SUCH HARDSHIP IN THAT FOREIGN LAND.
DID THEY DO ANYTHING BAD TO YOU?!
WHAT SORT OF PLACE DID YOU SLEEP IN? WAS IT A LIZARD-INFESTED CELLAR?
I HAVEN'T HAD JAPANESE FOOD IN SO LONG!
I'm so happy!

AMAMIZUKAN ONLY SURVIVED BECAUSE YOU SOLD YOURSELF INTO BONDAGE.
AND YET WE COULDN'T EVEN GO RESCUE YOU FROM SINGA-PORE, BECAUSE WE DON'T HAVE PASSPORTS...
SO WE WANTED TO GIVE YOU SUKIYAKI AS A SMALL TOKEN OF OUR APOLOGY... BUT...

...ALL WE HAD IN THE FRIDGE WAS CHOPPED PORK...
...SO IT'S PORK SUKI-YAKI!
Waaaaaah!
ZHOOP
AH!
NOW THAT WAS A GOOD BATH.
I feel great.
shing
I decided to borrow a shirt I found laying out to dry.
THANKS FOR LETTING ME TAKE ONE, TOO.

WHAT? D-DID YOU...
...BATHE TO-GETHER?!
AH!
NO, NO, WE TOOK TURNS!
Really they were together.
I WASHED MY BOSS'S BACK.

HANAMORI-SAN!! KURAKO MAY NOT LOOK IT, BUT SHE'S FEMALE!
EVEN IF SHE *IS* FLAT-CHESTED AND BONY AND HAS A PERSONALITY LIKE A MAN'S!!
I'M THE TYPE WHO DOESN'T WORRY ABOUT CHEST SIZE.
SHE JUST NEEDS TO BE SEXY.
HOW DARE YOU!
NO COED BATHING! AND BOYS AREN'T EVEN TECH-NICALLY ALLOWED HERE!
THAT'S RIGHT, EVEN IF YOU *DO* MANAGE TO GET IN BECAUSE YOU'RE CONVENIENT FOR DRIVING US PLACES AND YOU'VE GOT A VIBE LIKE THAT LAID-BACK SUNGLASSES GUY FROM THE ALFEE.

OH, WOW!
IT'S SUKI-YAKI!
Time to change the subject!
BUT IT'S PORK!
I WON'T EAT SUKIYAKI IF IT'S NOT BEEF.
HANAMORI, YOU GO HOME AND EAT BREAD.
AH, BANBA-SENPAI SHALL I GO BUY US SOME BREAD?
There's a Yamazaki Bakery nearby.
FORGET IT, JUST HELP SET THE TABLE.

YOU'RE RIGHT, I SHOULD BE TALKING ABOUT SOMETHING MORE IMPORTANT.
I'VE BROUGHT YOU ALL AN EXCELLENT PRESENT.
TA-DAH!
IT'S A GOD!!

WHY, LOOK AT THAT BUDDHA!
It's nice!!
I CAN'T BEAR TO SEE IT ANYMORE.
I THINK I'LL PUT IT IN THE LOBBY.
Oho.
They like this kind of thing.

FROM THIS DAY FORWARD, THIS IS YOUR GOD.
GOD!!
ARE YOU JUST HOPELESS OR WHAT?!
shwump

whisk whisk
カチャ カチャ
simmer simmer
ぐつ ぐつ
PORK JUST DOESN'T FEEL LIKE ENOUGH...
THE COMBINATION OF BEEF AND SHIRATAKI IS UNBEATABLE...
SIGH...
IF I ONLY HAD THAT MONEY FROM THE CASINO, I COULD GIVE EVERYONE SUKIYAKI WITH HIGH-GRADE JAPANESE BEEF...
Darn.

HEY, KURAKO. THE FIRST TIME YOU CAME HERE, YOU BROUGHT US MATSUSAKA BEEF.
GO TO YOUR DAD'S HOUSE AND GET US SOME AGAIN.
I want Nomu to try some.
AH, YES. THAT WAS QUITE GOOD MEAT!
Yep.
THAT BRINGS BACK MEMORIES...

...
NAH.

THE PORK TASTES PLENTY GOOD!
munch
ぱく

A SON OF THE KOIBUCHI FAMILY OF CONNOIS-SEURS, SAYING THAT?
SHALL I GO BUY SOME A5 BEEF WITH THE DIRTY MONEY YOUR FATHER HAS SQUEEZED OUT OF THE COM-MON FOLK?
Just hand me the gold card.
EXACTLY!
THAT'S OUR TAX MONEY !!!
ゆさ wobble
ゆさ wobble
NOT NECES-SARY.
I'VE DECIDED TO QUIT SPLURG-ING.

AND TO QUIT DEPENDING ON DAD'S MONEY, TOO!

WE'LL EAT THIS, AND THEN TOMORROW WE'RE BACK TO MAKING CLOTHES.

WE GOTTA BE READY, SO WE'LL BE OKAY WHENEVER THEY FINALLY KICK US OUT OF HERE.
OH, HEY.
GIMME AN EGG.
WHAT?
KICKED OUT...?
gloom
THAT CEO'S PROBABLY PISSED.
SEEING AS HOW I BROUGHT TSUKIMI BACK.
Y-YOU TOOK HER BACK BY FORCE, DIDN'T YOU?!
OF COURSE HE'S PISSED. AND HE OWNS THIS PLACE NOW, YOU KNOW.
WHO KNOWS WHAT'LL HAPPEN?
HE COULD SELL IT TO ANOTHER CONSTRUCTION FIRM, OR TEAR IT DOWN AND PUT UP AN AVIDY BUILDING HERE.
WELL, WHICH-EVER!
'CUZ THE POINT IS...
tonk
WE NEED TSUKIMI.
crack

WITHOUT HER, WE CAN'T CREATE ANYTHING.
THERE...
GAPE
あんぐり
whisk whisk
シャカシャカ
SWOON
フラ
GOD HELP US!!
IT'S A GOOD THING I BOUGHT THAT, HUH?
SKID
ズザア
DING-DONG
ピンポーン
HMM?
Who's that?

TSUKIMI-SAN...!

ER...
I HEARD THAT YOU WERE ABROAD...
WHAT MADE YOU GO SO SUD-DENLY?
OH! WELL...
...UM...
IT WAS... A CLOTHING THING...
...THAT CAME UP PRETTY SUD-DENLY...
I SEE.
WELL... I KNOW IT'S PRESUMP-TUOUS OF ME TO SAY THIS, BUT...

I-ITALY?

Y-Y-YOU WERE IN ITALY?

YES, JUST FOR THREE DAYS.

TH-THAT'S... A COUNTRY VERY FAR AWAY..

WAS IT A VACATION?

I-Italy...?

cough

Yeek...

...

TSUKIMI-SAN.

COULD I HAVE A BIT OF YOUR TIME TOMORROW?

nudge
I HAVE SOMETHING I'D LIKE TO GIVE YOU TOMORROW.
WILL THE CAFÉ AREA IN THE IMPERIAL HOTEL LOBBY AT 7:00 PM DO?
A very politician-like place to meet.
I-IS IT A SOUVENIR FROM ITALY...?
OH... SURE.
VERY WELL!
PLEASE BE SURE TO BE THERE!
PLEASE!
I'LL SEE YOU TOMOR-ROW, THEN!
DASH
blush
HUH?!
WAIT—

コポコポ
burble burble

We can't plan the budget or anything else until the concept is nailed down.

It's something completely different from the mass-produced stuff with simple lines that they make.

Jelly Fish's brand concept...

Tsukimi called the clothes they make "empty."
She also asked me, "Is that dress stylish?"
Drab people like me don't know what's stylish and what's not.

There must be plenty of girls like that in Japan.
Not just in Japan—worldwide.
We need a reason to put them in our clothes.
We can't sell our stuff until we make that clear.
If we start making clothes with nothing but momentum behind us, it'll just be a repeat of that exhibition.
Bottle: Premium Sake
Package: Dried, Salted Squid
COME ON!
AFTER-PARTY IN THE COURT-YARD!
ISN'T TSUKIMI READY YET?
WE'LL START DRINKING WHETHER THE GUEST OF HONOR IS HERE OR NOT!
troop troop
吟醸

HEY, KURAKO!
WE'RE GONNA GRILL SQUID ON THE CHARCOAL STOVE!
COME ON!!
HANAMORI-SAN PASSED OUT DRUNK.
He must be tired! I can't believe he's in the kitchen... on the floor...
pitter
patter

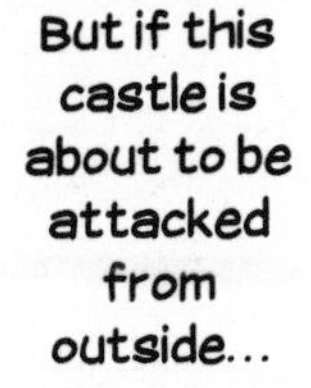

...and destroyed...

...then they'll be forced to shame themselves in the outside world for the first time.
...
LISTEN.
IF THIS PLACE WERE GONE...
...YOU WOULDN'T BE ABLE TO GRILL DRIED SQUID IN THOSE SWEATS AND TRACK SUITS.
WHAT'S YOUR PROB-LEM?
WHY ARE YOU RAINING ON OUR PARADE?
I'M SAYING, IF—NO, IT'S NOT AN *IF* ANYMORE.
WHEN YOU'RE KICKED OUT OF HERE AND YOU EACH HAVE TO LIVE ALONE AND WORK OUT THERE IN THE WORLD...
...WHICH MEANS YOU'LL BE IN A POSITION WHERE YOU HAVE TO PUT TOGETHER SOME HALFWAY-DECENT OUTFITS...

...YOU WON'T BE ABLE TO DRESS LIKE THAT ANYMORE, RIGHT?

IT'LL BE FINE. I'LL GET A PART-TIME JOB TYING SHEAVES OF SUGAR CANE IN A FIELD ON ISHIGAKI ISLAND.

crackle crackle パチパチ

LIS-TEN.

IF YOU HAD TO GO OUT IN SOCIETY, HYPOTHETICALLY, WHAT KIND OF CLOTHES WOULD YOU WANT TO WEAR?

skrut ガタ

...SETTING PRICE ASIDE FOR NOW.

WHAT KIND OF CLOTHES WOULD YOU BE ***WILLING*** TO WEAR?

...

...
EASY ONES...
...THAT ARE DU-RABLE...
...AND DON'T STAND OUT...
GREAT.
GIVE ME MORE!
YOU TOO, CHIEKO-SAN AND NOMU-SAN!

CLOTHES THAT DON'T COMPRESS MY STOMACH, SO I CAN EAT A LOT OF FOOD IN THEM...
ONES WHOSE COLORS DON'T FADE IN THE WASH...
I wear my kimono loose around the waist, truth be told.
ONES THAT AREN'T MAGGOT-LIKE...

ONES I CAN WEAR YEAR-ROUND!!
Like this track suit.
OHO, THEY'RE GETTING INTO THIS.
I WANT TO GET BY WITH JUST TWO SETS, DAMMIT!

OKAY, I GOT IT!
I GET THE PRACTI-CALITY ANGLE!
SO...

WHAT ABOUT THE DESIGN?

FOR EXAMPLE...

...SUPPOSE YOU'RE AT YOUR JOB...

...AND ONE OF YOUR COWORKERS IS GETTING MARRIED.

YOU MIGHT GET INVITED TO THE WEDDING RECEPTION, RIGHT?

CHIEKO-SAN WOULD BE OKAY, SINCE SHE'S GOT A KIMONO...

...BUT WHAT ABOUT THE REST OF YOU?

YES, THANK GOODNESS. *I'm a winner.*

I WOULDN'T GO.

THE OUTSIDE WORLD DOESN'T LET YOU GET AWAY WITH THAT!

THEN...

I...

...WOULD WEAR THE SAME CLOTHES TO THE WEDDING RECEPTION.

YES.

ME, TOO.

IT'S A WASTE OF MONEY TO BUY NEW CLOTHES, AFTER ALL.

Hah.

EVEN IF I'M NOT A STYLISH, AS LONG AS MY CLOTHES DON'T SEEM WEIRD, THAT'S ENOUGH...

SO IF THERE WERE A DESIGN THAT WOULD WORK THAT WAY, WOULD YOU BUY IT EVEN IF IT WERE A *TINY BIT* EXPENSIVE?
...
YES.
PERSON-ALLY, I WOULD.

IF THAT DESIGN WOULD SPARE ME THE PAIN OF LOOKING FOR A NEW OUTFIT EACH TIME IN THAT GIANT DEPARTMENT STORE...

...THEN I'D BUY IT, I THINK.

HMM...
WHAT DO I WEAR TOMORROW?
トボトボ
trudge trudge

I CAN'T GO TO THE IMPERIAL HOTEL DRESSED LIKE **THIS**...
...AND I FEEL LIKE A JELLYFISH DRESS WOULD BE TOO FLASHY...

WILL WE BE EATING THERE?
I'M STUMPED ...

I'LL HAVE TO GET KURANOSUKE-SAN TO PICK OUT MY CLOTHES AGAIN...

How long am I going to lean on Kuranosuke-san like this?

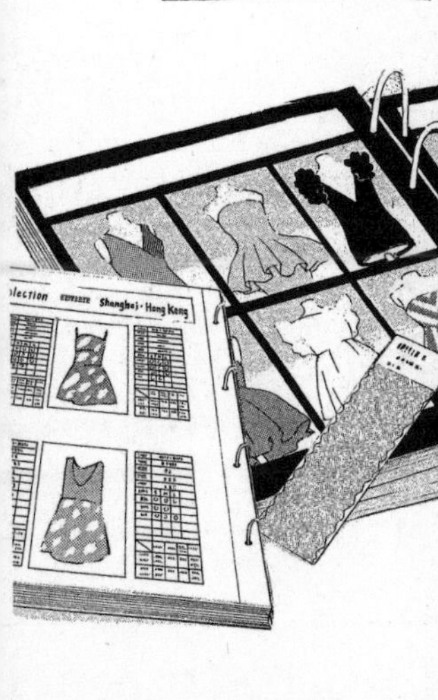
I went all the way to Singapore, and I had to study clothes all day there.
Shanghai - Hong Kong

But...
I can't believe that after all that, I still can't decide what to wear outside the house.
...I think there must be lots of girls like me.
Girls who don't know what they should wear tomorrow.

If I could get girls like that to wear Jelly Fish's clothes...

Apparel Industry Strateg
1. What measures/strategies will you adopt?
*Bargain and discount sales
カタカタ
taka taka
snore
クカー
カタカタ

TEITO HOTEL
THIS SHIRT SHOULD BE OKAY... RIGHT?

I APOLOGIZE FOR ASKING YOU HERE TODAY WHEN YOU MUST BE BUSY...
NOT AT ALL.
I-IT'S GOOD OF YOU TO SHARE THIS LOVELY THREE-TIERED CAKE SET WITH ME...
WELL.
...THEN.
THE ITEM I WANTED TO GIVE YOU...
...IS...
rummage ゴソ

...WELL...

POK パカ

...THIS!

ZHOOP ズイ

TSUKIMI-SAN.

YES?

IT'S A RING.

...
I KNOW.
SHFF
I'LL...
...JUST PUT IT...
HUH?!
SHFF
WHA ...?
TSUKIMI-SAN.
WILL YOU...

...MARRY
ME?
PLEASE?

Episode 80

Shall We Marry?

Tsukimi...
All girls can be beautiful princesses when they grow up.
When you grow up and get married...
...I'll make you a white lace wedding dress, just like this jelly.

When you get married...
Mar-ried...
Marr...
...ied?

TSUKIMI-SAN, WILL YOU MARRY ME?
LET'S GET MARRIED AND BUILD A HAPPY HOME TOGETHER.
PLEASE DON'T GO FAR AWAY WITHOUT TELLING ME AGAIN.
NO...
I MEAN...
...PLEASE DON'T EVER LEAVE MY SIDE AGAIN.

I PROMISE TO PROTECT YOU.
...
ビクッ flinch
ガタ skrut
HUH?!
...
...
UM...

scoot
ズ
OH, NO!
WAIT!
TSUKI—
skrut
ガタッ
ズッ… ズズズズ
scoot scoot scoot
DON'T—
DON'T BE SCARED!
IT'S OKAY!
IT'S REALLY OKAY!
scoot scoot

I... I'M SORRY...
CAN I... UM...
C- C-C- CAN I...

CAN I...!
...T-TAKE SOME TIME TO THINK ABOUT THIS?

WHAT ?!
OH!
Y- YOU'D... LIKE TO...
... THINK ?!

I...
...REALLY HOPE THAT'S...
... OKAY.
OH...
OH, I SEE...

OH... ...OKAY THEN.
P- PLEASE...
...TAKE SOME TIME TO THINK...

DASH
ACK!
AUGH ...
AH...
AAAH ...
HUFF
HUFF

ドタタタタタタ
tmp
tmp
tmp
tmp
tmp

MAMA!
LOOK, THAT LADY RUNS REALLY FAST!
SHE MUST DREAM OF BEING IN THE OLYMPICS.
ドダダダ
tmp tmp tmp

KEKKON? BLOOD-STAIN?*
*In Japanese, "kekkon" can mean wedding or bloodstain.
KEKKON ...
wheeze
wheeze
KEK-KON?
WHERE WAS THE BLOOD-STAIN, TSUKIMI?
huff huff
KEKKON!!
BANG
WHAM
WHERE'S THE MURDER SCENE?!?!
A SUDDEN VIOLENT MURDER IN OUR PEACE-FUL LITTLE CITY!
trot trot trot

AH!
HERE IT IS.
NWAAH!
fwoop
wobble
TH-THIS IS...
WAIT, "BLOOD-STAIN"?
THIS IS JUST A PER-SIMMON FALLEN FROM A TREE...
stare
ぐちゃっ
splurch
NO, IT'S BLOOD!
Mayaya boldly decides to go all in.
CALL THE CSIS!
CSIS?
CSI KURAKO KOIBUCHI IS ON THE SCENE!!
USE THIS BLOODSTAIN TO PROFILE THE PERP FOR US.
Woo!
AHA!
LISTEN, THE NEIGH-BORHOOD CAN SEE US OUT HERE, SO WHY DON'T WE KEEP THE GAMES INSIDE, OKAY?

BUT TSUKIMI!
TSUKIMI CAME RUNNING HOME PALE AS A GHOST...
...SCREAMING "BLOOD-STAIN! BLOOD-STAIN!"
NATURALLY WE ASSUMED THE WORST.
twitch
ピク
SCREAM-ING?
KEK-KON?
Is that right?
CORRECT! THIS IS THE VIC'S BLOOD!
THE VIC IS SHIBUO KAKITA, 40 YEARS OLD.
LOOKS LIKE HE WAS PUSHED TO HIS DEATH FROM SOMEPLACE PRETTY HIGH UP.
swivel
KEKKON?
FLINCH
天水館
天水館

PWAP
...
SO...
WHAT'S WITH THAT GIANT RING...?
HUH ?!
UM!
I...
THIS IS...
NO WAY...
DON'T TELL ME...
YOU'RE WEARING IT ON YOUR LEFT HAND. DON'T TELL ME...
...THAT MEANS...

...MY BROTHER PROPOSED TO YOU?
FOR REAL?
...
PRO...
天水館
天水館
PRO...
...
POS...
PRO...
SHOW ME THAT RING.

*Founder and emperor of the Qin Dynasty.

WOW.
ALL THAT LAUGHING MADE ME THIRSTY.
くる swivel
CHIEKO-SAN! TEA, PLEASE!
What a riot.
スタスタ stride stride
Phew...
KURA-NOSUKE-SAN...

ARE YOU AN IDIOT, SHU?
WHY DIDN'T YOU COME TO ME FOR ADVICE FIRST?
I ought to deck you.
WELL... I THOUGHT SOONER WAS BETTER, AND I ENDED UP RUSHING THINGS...
tha-dum tha-dum
WHEN AND WHERE DID YOU PRO-POSE?
TODAY ...
...JUST NOW...
...IN THE CAFÉ AREA OF THE IMPERIAL HOTEL LOBBY...
WHAT WERE YOUR EXACT WORDS?
"WILL YOU MARRY ME?"
"LET'S BUILD A HAPPY HOME TO-GETHER."
YEAH.
I GIVE YOU A 2 OUT OF 10.
Or there-abouts.
MAYBE I...
... SHOULD'VE DONE IT...
...AT THE AQUA-RIUM...
... AFTER ALL.
YES. YOU SHOULD HAVE DONE IT AFTER DARK, AT THE AQUARIUM.
A CAFÉ IN A HOTEL LOBBY IS WHERE YOU MEET UP TO CELEBRATE THE SIXTIETH BIRTHDAY OF SOMEONE YOU WENT TO TAIMEI ELEMENTARY SCHOOL WITH, NOT WHERE YOU PRO-POSE.
NNGH ...
BUT...

I REALLY FELT LIKE...
...AT THE AQUARIUM, IN FRONT OF THE JELLYFISH TANKS...
...I WOULDN'T BE ABLE TO DO IT.
...
WHY NOT?
WELL...
I DIDN'T THINK I COULD GET HER TO LOOK AT ME.
WITH JELLY-FISH...
...SWIMMING RIGHT IN FRONT OF HER LIKE THAT...
...I JUST FIG-URED...
...SHE'D BE SPELL-BOUND BY THEM...

...AND SHE WOULDN'T LISTEN TO A WORD I SAID.
I SUPPOSE I'M AFRAID.
BE-CAUSE...
...IT FEELS LIKE SHE'LL DISAPPEAR ON ME AGAIN.

...
SHU-SAN...
...
HA HA.

I'M...
...PRETTY PATHETIC, HUH?
DOES YOUR FATHER... DOES KOIBUCHI-SENSEI KNOW?
OF COURSE NOT.
THIS IS MY PROB-LEM.

I KNOW BETTER THAN MOST WHAT IT MEANS TO MARRY INTO A POLITICAL FAMILY.
TSUKIMI-SAN WOULD BE IN FOR A WORLD OF TROUBLE.
I'LL ONLY TELL MY FATHER AFTER WE'RE BOTH FIRMLY RESOLVED TO MARRY EACH OTHER.
BECAUSE I'M CERTAIN THAT HE'D BE AGAINST IT AT THIS STAGE.

WELL, THEN!
shing
I STILL HAVE A LOT TO DO TODAY.
I'D BETTER SHAKE OFF THIS MOOD.
YES.
I'LL SEE YOU LATER, SIR.
HIYA, HANAMORI!
BEEN A DEV-DEV-DEVIL OF A LONG TIME!
IT'S DEVILISH PM NEGISHI!
SHU-SAN PROPOSED TO A COMMONER WOMAN.
HA-WHAA?!
HMM?
WAIT.
WHAT DID I JUST SAY?
THAT SHU-SHU PROPOSED TO A PLAIN JAPANESE JANE!
THAT'S WHAT!

CAN I TELL SHU PAPA? I MEAN, I'M THE UNCLE, I GOTTA SAY SOMETHING!
WELL, NO ONE CAN STOP TONGUES FROM WAGGING.

HUH...
THAT'S WEIRD...
I SWORE TO MYSELF I WOULDN'T BLAB THIS TIME.
And it was a serious moment, too... Why did I do that?
?
OMG, WHAT A SCOOP!

I ASSUME THEY CAN OVERCOME ANY OBSTACLE, IF THEY LOVE EACH OTHER.
If they can't, it wasn't meant to be.
PERFECT! I'M MEETING SHU PAPA FOR TEA AFTER THE PLENARY SESSION!
Maybe I'll let it slip!

プカ
bob bob
プカ

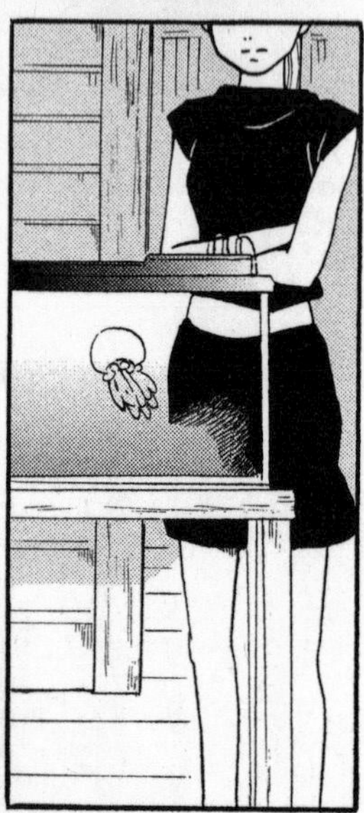

OH, HELLO, KURAKO.
YOU CAME AT A GOOD TIME— I WAS JUST ABOUT TO SLICE UP SOME CASTELLA CAKE.
HEY...

IS THIS JELLY...
...A BOY OR A GIRL?
WHAT?
HOW SHOULD I KNOW?
ASK TSUKIMI!
WAIT, WHERE *IS* TSUKIMI?!
WELL... SHE'S BEEN HOLED UP IN HER ROOM SINCE SHE GOT HOME...
OH, DEAR!
TSUKIMIIII! WE HAVE CASTELLA!
DO YOU WANT BLACK TEA OR GREEN TEA?
ドドタタ
clomp clomp
SHU, YOU ASS...
WHY?
WHY NOW, OF ALL TIMES?

WHAT NOW?
WHAT NOW?
WHAT NOW?
WHAT...
...NOW?

WHAT NOW...?
plop

Shu asked me...
...to marry him.
He meant "marry" as in *marry*.
Kekkon.
Marriage.

But...
It's me.
Marriage exists in such a different world from mine...
...it doesn't feel real at all.
Mom...
I...
I loved Shu.
I know I did.
That time...
And that time...
And that time...
I did, so...
why?
Why am I confused right now?

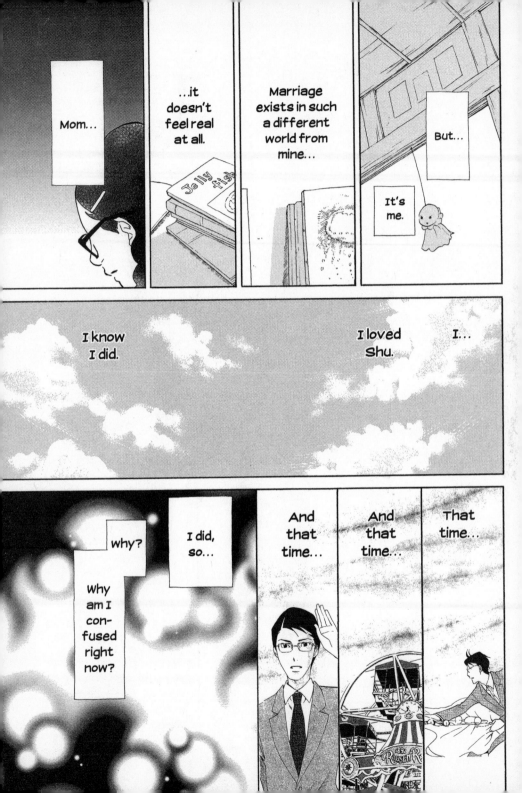

A normal girl would be happy to hear those words, right?
I've seen it over and over in TV shows and manga.
When the man proposes, the woman always cries with happiness.
So how come I'm not crying?
最新クラゲ図鑑
Book: The Latest Guide to Jellyfish
When I was a kid, you told me...
...that when I got married, you'd make me a wedding dress that looked just like that jelly.
But...
...a girl like me wouldn't look right in a frilly, showy dress like that.
Because that's a princess's dress.

Those only look right on Kura-nosuke.

The best I could do...

...would be this.

flip パラ...

No, not even that.

Planula

ertilized Egg

New Polyp

eneration

tted Jelly

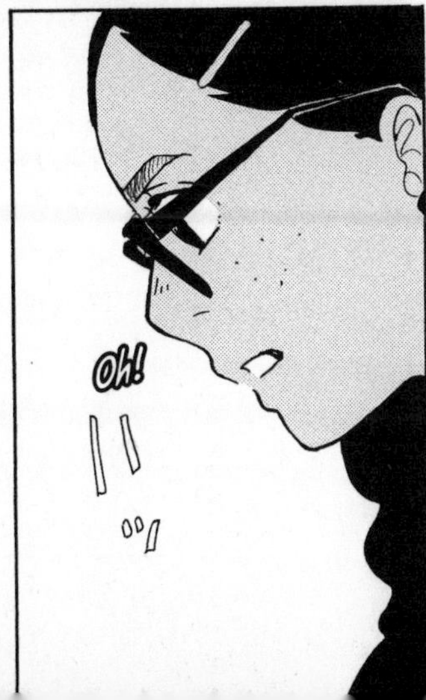

OHO.
FEEDING THE JELLYFISH YOURSELF IS A KIND GESTURE, KURAKO.
HEY...
CLARA IS FEMALE, RIGHT?
"CLARA" IS A GIRL'S NAME, ANYWAY.
HUH...
DO JELLYFISH HAVE SEXES?
JIJI-SAN, LOOK IT UP FOR US.
HMM ...
IT LOOKS LIKE THEY DO...
taka taka
WOW.
WHO KNEW?
SO CLARA'S A GIRL, BUT SHE'LL SPEND HER WHOLE LIFE IN THIS TANK WITHOUT EVER GETTING MARRIED OR HAVING A BOYFRIEND?
ACTUALLY, DO JELLIES LAY EGGS?
PROBABLY NOT EGGS. HOW *DO* THEY REPRODUCE?
FRAGMENTATION, MAYBE?
NO, IT LOOKS LIKE THERE'S A SORT OF EGG... OR EMBRYO? BUT...
HUH?!
WHAT? WHAT?!
IT SAYS HERE THAT THE EGG ATTACHES TO THE SEA FLOOR OR A ROCK WHERE IT GROWS LIKE A TINY SEA ANEMONE...
A-ANEMONE?
WHY? I DON'T GET IT.
HOW DO THEY START SWIMMING AFTER THAT?

LET'S SEE...
THEY'RE STIMULATED BY CHANGES IN ENVIRONMENT, LIKE WHEN THE WATER TEMPERATURE CHANGES WITH THE SEASONS...
...AND THE WEIRD LITTLE ANEMONE THING HAS A METAMORPHOSIS OR SOMETHING TO CHANGE FORMS.
BWA HA HA! WEIRDO!
AND THEN...
...IT STARTS BEING A FLOATING CREATURE.
THAT'S WHAT IT SAYS.

HA HA, THAT'S COOL!
THEY'RE JUST LIKE YOU GUYS.
tump tump tump tump
ダダダダダ

ダダダダダ
TUMP TUMP TUMP

KURANO-SUKE-SAN!
...
TSUKI-MI!

JEL-LIES...
...CHANGE FORMS...!
最クラゲ図鑑

YEAH...
"METAMOR-PHOSIS," RIGHT?

JELLY FISH'S BRAND CONCEPT.
I JUST FIGURED IT OUT.
TSUKIMI.
META-MOR-PHOSIS!
YES!
YOU NEED BOTH FORMS— IT DEPENDS ON THE DAY.
JUST LIKE THE ANEMONE THINGS CHANGING INTO JELLIES.
YOU HAVE PRINCESS DAYS...
...AND WARRIOR WOMAN DAYS...
...AND DAYS WHEN YOU JUST WANT TO STAY HOME.
CLOTHES FOR GIRLS WHO WANT TO METAMOR-PHOSE.
IT'S *METAMORPHOSIS.*

TSUKIMI...
クラゲ図鑑
THIS IS NO TIME FOR YOU TO BE GETTING MARRIED.
天水館

Episode 81

The Dangerous Lives of Koibuchi Boys

Jellyfish radically change forms as they mature.

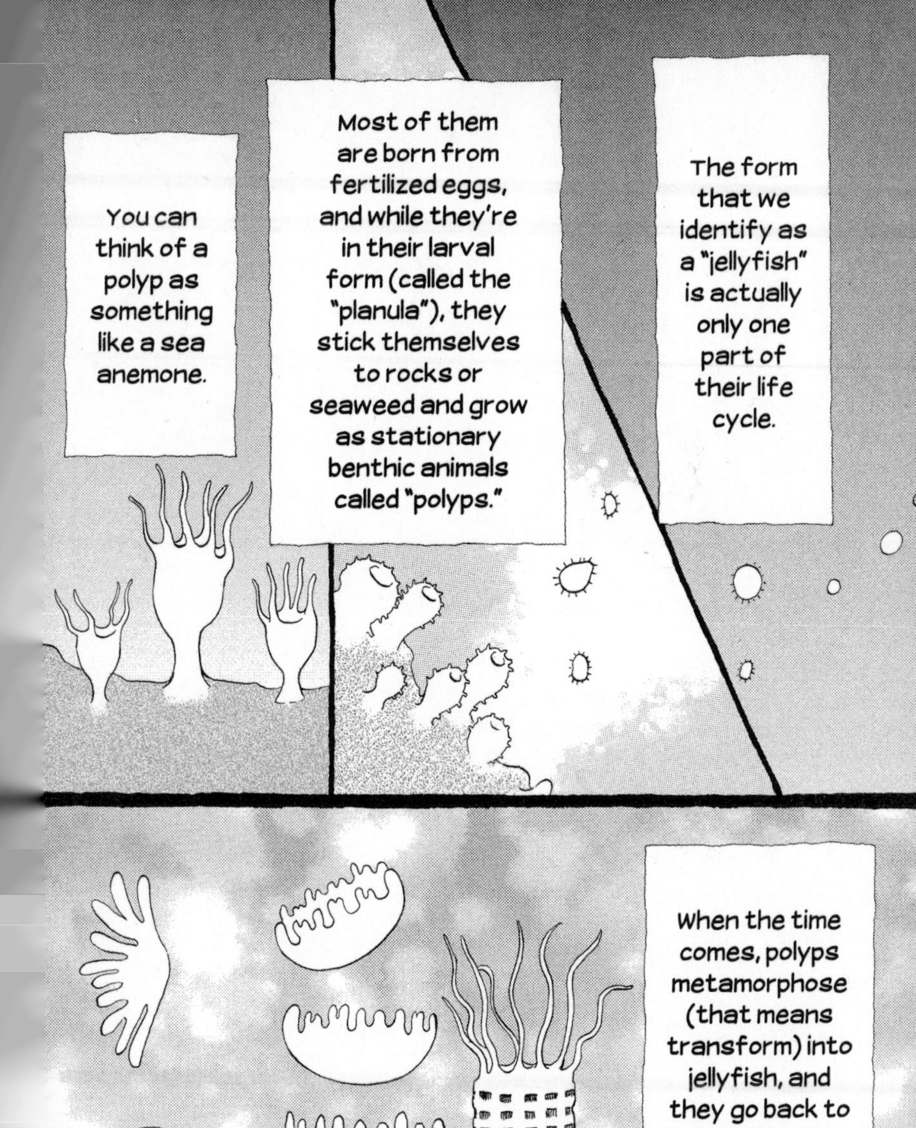
The form that we identify as a "jellyfish" is actually only one part of their life cycle.
Most of them are born from fertilized eggs, and while they're in their larval form (called the "planula"), they stick themselves to rocks or seaweed and grow as stationary benthic animals called "polyps."
You can think of a polyp as something like a sea anemone.
When the time comes, polyps metamorphose (that means transform) into jellyfish, and they go back to living a floating life as plankton.

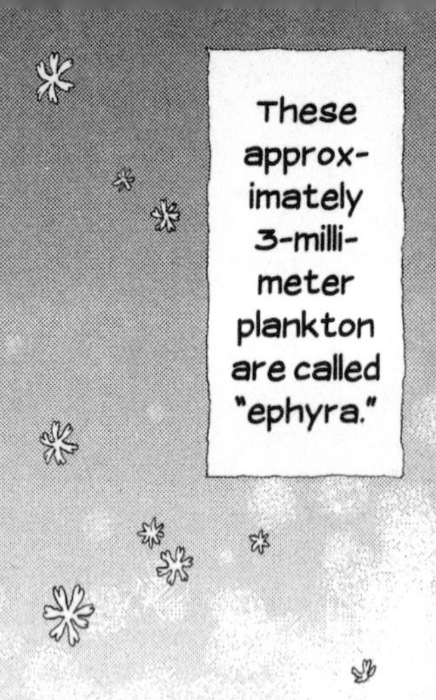
These approximately 3-millimeter plankton are called "ephyra."

Ephyra are baby jellyfish shaped like flowers.

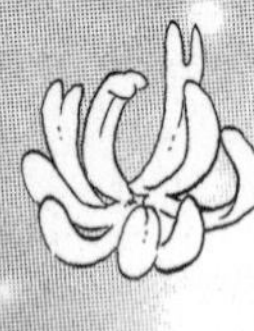
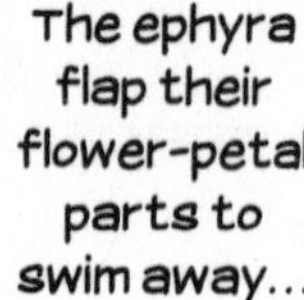

The ephyra flap their flower-petal parts to swim away…

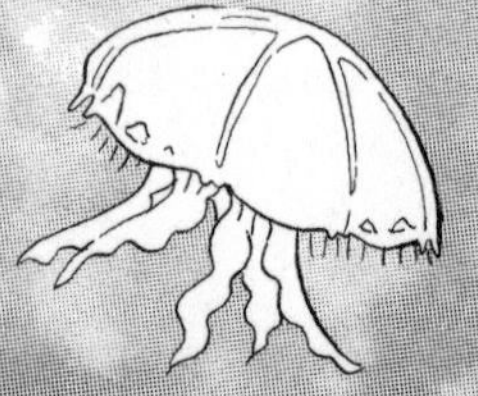
…and as they eat more prey, they grow from the flower shape into a circle shape, which is when they become young "jellyfish" with the same form they'll have as adults.

...THEN THESE YOUNG JELLYFISH KEEP GROWING WITHOUT CHANGING SHAPE ANYMORE!

THAT'S THE CYCLE OF JELLYFISH METAMOR-PHOSIS.

ZHOOP
ガラ
YOU CLOWNS GOT THAT MEMO-RIZED?!

JELLY-FISH START OUT AS ANEMO-NES!
THE SHOCKING TRUTH!
WELL? BET YOU DIDN'T KNOW *THAT*, EH?

ACTUALLY... I DON'T UNDER-STAND ANY OF IT...
WHAT STRANGE CREA-TURES...
LIKE WARRING STATES GENER-ALS WHO COME OF AGE AND JUST KEEP CHANG-ING NAMES ...
Ephyra?
Planula?

RIGHT THEN!
WE'RE RESTARTING JELLY FISH!
FIRST, WE CLEAN THE ATELIER!
GOTTA PREP SO WE'LL BE READY TO BEGIN WORK AT ANY TIME!!
WHAT?!

JIJI-SAMA, YOU GO TO NISHA'S AND ASK ABOUT FABRIC PURCHASES!
NOMU-SAN, YOU GET READY TO MAKE PATTERNS!
AH... OKAY.
HUH?
AND TSUKIMI...
...STARTING TODAY, YOU'RE GONNA HOLE UP IN YOUR ROOM AND CRANK OUT DESIGNS!
WAIT ...
WAIT A SEC...
A MO-MENT...
PLEASE GIVE ME PERMIS-SION...
...TO GO OUT FOR JUST A MOMENT!
OH, REAL-LY!
GO OUT WHERE?!
"WHERE"?
UM...
YOU KNOW ...
I...

I... NEED TO GO TALK WITH SHU-SAN...
...DON'T I?
FINE, I'LL GO WITH YOU AND YELL AT HIM.
I'LL TELL HIM, "WEDDINGS, PROPOSALS, THAT WEIRD-ASS ENGAGEMENT RING..."
"ALL OF IT IS REVOLTING, YOU STUPID VIRGIN!"
THAT'LL TEACH HIM!
Graaah!
COME ON, LET'S GO. THE DIET'S NOT IN SESSION TODAY, SO HE MIGHT BE LOAFING AROUND AT HOME.
W-W-WAIT, PLEASE!
WAIT!
WAIT!
thwap
thwap
I-IT'S ALL RIGHT. I CAN GO BY MYSELF!

HUH?
THIS ISN'T...!
THIS ISN'T THE KIND OF THING...
...THAT IT'S OKAY TO TROUBLE YOU WITH, KURANOSUKE.
I'LL BE BACK!
IN AN HOUR—NO, 45 MINUTES!
SO, UM...
PLEASE LET ME GO ALONE!
UNFAIR, TSUKIMI! YOU WANT TO SKIP OUT ON THE HARD WORK THE REST OF US FACE, DON'T YOU?
I'D SKIP THE CLEANING TOO IF I COULD, AND TAKE THE RED ARROW TO CHICHIBU OR SOME-THING.
HURRY UP AND PUT ON THIS SMOCK.
Always best to wear one for cleaning.
I'M SORRY, EVERYONE! I'LL BE BACK SOON!
SURE, SLACKER!

...

huff
huff

WILL YOU MARRY ME?
PLEASE?

What should I say?

What words...

...will make Shu-san understand how I feel?

I barely understand these feelings myself.

huff

huff

HMM?
TSUKIMI-SAN?

JERK
WHAT ?!
gulp

I...
I'M SO SORRY TO... BARGE IN ON YOU AT HOME...
...LIKE SOME SUSPICIOUS PERSON...
NOT AT ALL!
I'M HONORED. THANK YOU FOR COMING!

P-P-P-PLEASE, COME IN. I'LL MAKE TEA...
BETTER NOT. YOUR PARENTS ARE BOTH HOME RIGHT NOW.
Ow!
Oh, and I think Baldy's here.
TSUKI-MI-SAN!
DASH
OH... SHE RAN.
Wah!
WAIT, WAIT, WAIT!
TMP
TMP
TMP
TMP

GRAB
PLEASE ...
...WAIT...
squeeze
BLUSH
In Tsukimi's Mind
squish
!!!
WHAP
Oh!
I...!
I'M SO SORRY! I SHOULD NEVER TOUCH A WOMAN WITHOUT PERMI—
N-NO!
THAT'S NOT IT!
IT'S JUST, MY ARM IS LIKE A NEW YEAR'S HAM...
I COULDN'T LET YOU TOUCH HAM.

I'M VERY SORRY FOR SAYING SOMETHING LIKE THAT SO SUDDENLY YESTERDAY.
ZERO POINTS!
OUT HERE IN THE STREET?
YOU'RE ASKING HER AGAIN?
NO WAY.
WHA?
0 pts
TSUKIMI-SAN, WH-WH-WHAT'S YOUR ANSWER TO MY PROPOSAL?!
HAM-WHAT?!
BUT, WELL, MAY I ASK WHETHER YOU'VE GIVEN THE MATTER DUE CONSIDERATION SINCE THEN?!
UM, YES!
I...
I-I DON'T KNOW ABOUT "DUE CONSIDERATION," BUT...
I...
I DID THINK ABOUT IT.

YOU SEE...
...I HAVEN'T MANAGED TO ACCOMPLISH ANYTHING YET.
I MEAN...
...I KNOW SOMEONE LIKE ME MIGHT NOT BE ABLE TO DO MUCH OF ANYTHING, BUT...
BUT...
I STILL HAVE MORE THINGS I WANT TO MAKE.
I STILL WANT TO DO NEW THINGS...

WITH KURANOSUKE?

YOU WANT TO DO THEM WITH KURANOSUKE?

KURANOSUKE-SAN IS MY PRINCESS.

...

KU...

SO I...

I WANT MY FRIENDS AND I...

...TO KEEP MAKING DRESSES FOR KURANOSUKE-SAN TO WEAR...

BUT THE THING IS, TO ME, *YOU* WERE THE PRINCESS.
HA HA...
IT'S ALL TOO BACK-WARDS NOT TO LAUGH.

WE'RE A FUNNY PAIR.
UH-OH.
SHE LEFT.
UH-OH. SHU'S KNEES GAVE OUT.
A BRAVE BUT FAILED ATTEMPT?
A BRAVE BUT FAILED ATTEMPT.

PHEW. THANK GOODNESS.
THE GIRL'S IN HER RIGHT MIND.
YES.
THIS IS NO FAMILY FOR SOMEONE SO CHILDLIKE TO MARRY INTO.
What a relief!
SHE'S FAR TOO YOUNG.
I HOPE SHU-SHU IS OKAY.
HE'S SUCH AN IDIOT. Truly.
HE'S TOO PURE—I DON'T THINK HE'S CUT OUT TO BE A POLITICIAN.

CLEAN LIKE YOU MEAN IT! THE *JOUNETSU TAIRIKU* NEWS CREW COULD BE IN HERE WITH THEIR CAMERAS AT ANY TIME!

IN YOUR DREAMS, YOU COUNTER OF UNHATCHED CHICKENS!

YOU POULTRY DREAM-ER!

Graaah!

LOOK, A THREE KINGDOMS CAPSULE TOY.

I'LL GET IT!!

SKID

THIS IS JUST AN EGG-SHELL!
UGH, WHO TOSSED AN EGGSHELL ON THE FLOOR?
WE WERE ALWAYS EATING CHICKEN RAMEN HERE DURING OUR ALL-NIGHTERS BEFORE THE FASHION SHOW...
WHEN I THINK THAT HELL IS ABOUT TO START AGAIN...
DANG, NOW I WANT RAMEN.
BREAK TIME!
WHAT?! AL-READY?
IT'S TIME FOR THE AFTER-NOON NEWS.
tunk
tunk
I NEED AN EGG OVER HERE!
SHEESH. MAKE SURE YOU WORK AF-TER YOU EAT!
AND I'M EATING, TOO!
A WEEK HAS PASSED...
...SINCE PRICES ON CHINA'S SHANG-HAI STOCK EXCHANGE PLUM-METED LAST MONDAY, AND THE DECLINE SHOWS NO SIGNS OF STOPPING.
slurp slurp

I'M YOSHIOKA, REPORTING FROM THE SHANGHAI BUREAU.
THIS "CHINESE BLACK MONDAY" HAS DEALT MASSIVE DAMAGE TO FOREIGN-OWNED ENTERPRISES IN THE CHINESE MARKET.
FOR EXAMPLE, TAKE THIS FLAGSHIP CLOTHING STORE, RUN BY A SINGAPORE APPAREL COMPANY.
AVIDY
BUSINESS HERE HAS FALLEN OFF SINCE BLACK MONDAY, AND SALES FIGURES ARE IN A NOSEDIVE.
WHAT ?!
WHAT ?!
HOLD ON...
TURN UP THE VOLUME!
HUH ?!
SALES AREN'T THE ONLY PROBLEM. THIS STOCK DROP HAS TRIGGERED A SIGNIFICANT LOSS IN FOREIGN COMPANIES' MARKET CAPITALIZATION, AND EXPERTS FEAR THAT THIS COULD INFLUENCE INTERNATIONAL MARKETS INTO THE NEXT WEEK.

THAT...
...WAS AVIDY ON THE SCREEN JUST NOW, RIGHT?
HMM?
I WASN'T WATCHING.
slurp slurp
ズズズ
MAYAYA! IT WAS, RIGHT?!
HAVE YOU GOT THE EGGS YET, CHIEKO?!
FOR REAL?
"CHINESE BLACK MONDAY"...?

...
WELL, DRAT.
R Z
P V

CHINA'S BUBBLE BURST MUCH SOONER THAN I EXPECTED IT TO.

W-WELL, SIR, FIRST WE CAN SHIFT ALL OUR CAPITAL AVIDY MERCHANDISE TO LITTLE AVIDY IN SHANGHAI AND HONG KONG...
I'LL PUT THE BAN-GLADESH FACTORY RELOCA-TION TEM-PORARILY ON HOLD.
I SUPPOSE A LITTLE STOPGAP RISK HEDGING LIKE THAT IS BETTER THAN NOTHING.
S-SIR!
IF I MAY...
IF WE PUT THE BAN-GLADESH FACTORY ON HOLD...

...WE'LL TAKE A HEAVY LOSS ON ALL THE RAW FABRIC WE BOUGHT UP FOR NEXT SEASON.
NOT TO MENTION THE FACTORY WORKERS' FRUSTRATIONS WILL EXPLODE AGAIN!!
BETTER TO GET RID OF RAW FABRIC THAN BURN OUR GOODS AFTER WE'VE PUT IN THE COST OF MANUFACTURING.

AT ANY RATE...
...AT LEAST LAY THE GROUNDWORK SO THAT WE CAN SHUT DOWN OUR DIRECTLY-MANAGED STORES IN CHINA AND PULL OUT AT A MOMENT'S NOTICE.
B-BUT SIR...
WE HAVE OVER A HUNDRED FULL-TIME EMPLOYEES IN SHANGHAI ALONE!
IF WE PULL OUT, THEY'LL...

DO YOU INTEND TO LET SOME MISPLACED SENTIMENT DRAG YOU RIGHT DOWN ALONG WITH THE CHINESE STOCK MARKET?
IF WE DON'T MAKE BACK THESE LOSSES NEXT SEASON, IT'LL START AFFECTING OUR SINGAPORE STORES, TOO.
WHAT ARE YOU TWO TALKING ABOUT?
CUT THEM.
CUT ANY WASTE YOU FIND.
YOUR JOB IS TO THINK ABOUT SAVING THE TREE, EVEN IF YOU HAVE TO CUT OFF ALL THE BRANCHES TO DO IT.

CHINESE CHURCH
禮拜堂
FAYONG.
LOOK HOW MANY TOWELS SOMEONE DONATED.
OH!
THAT'S WONDERFUL—THE CHILDREN'S TOWELS WERE GETTING OLD.
I'LL SWAP THESE IN RIGHT NOW.
PERFECT, THANK YOU.
pad pad pad
WOW!

THESE TOWELS ARE SO WHITE AND FLUFFY!
THEY'RE NEW TOWELS!
So fluffy!
THAT'S RIGHT. THEY WERE DONATED.
YOU REALLY USED THIS TOWEL A LONG TIME...
IT'S TATTERED AND COMING APART IN PLACES...
WILL YOU THROW IT AWAY?
NOPE.
MAYBE I'LL CUT IT DOWN INTO DISHRAGS FOR CLEANING THE TABLES.
WE USED TO DO THAT HERE...
...IN MY DAY.

Metamor-
phosis.
Changing
forms, like
jellies...
Changing
appear-
ances...
Clothing
that's born
from a single
cloth and then
transforms.
I'm
counting
on you,
Tsukimi.
I know
you can
do it.
In fact,
you're
the only
one who
can.

We can't win against him unless it's with clothes that only we can make.

IT'S A GOD!!

Episode 0
On the Eve of the Cross-Dressing

Why did I start cross-dressing, you ask?
It all began during the fall of my last year in high school.

DAD.

I GOT IN.

W.U., JUST LIKE YOU WANTED.

YOU DID IT! CONGRATULATIONS.
I KNEW YOU WERE SMART.

NAH, I JUST SKIPPED THE LINE.
PLUS DAD USED HIS CONNECTIONS.
SO, COME APRIL, YOU'LL BE A COLLEGE STUDENT...

WOW...
OUR KURANOSUKE, A COLLEGE STUDENT...
AT W.U. ...
squeak squeak
キュッ キュッ

THE GIRLS WILL BE ALL OVER YOU, AND YOU'LL GO THROUGH THEM ALL.
YOUR SEX LIFE WILL BE GREAT!
I DUNNO ABOUT GOING THROUGH THEM ALL, BUT YOU'RE PROBABLY RIGHT ABOUT THE FIRST PART.
lurch
スクッ

YOU'RE ON YOUR WAY TO SCHOOL, RIGHT?
WANT A RIDE?
HUH?!
REALLY? THAT'D BE GREAT!

VROOM

A boring home.

A boring life.

And a boring …

…me.

WHERE'S SHU TODAY?

HE WENT TO SHIZUOKA THIS MORNING FOR A SUPPORTERS' ORGANIZATION MEETING.

YOUR FATHER EXPECTS GREAT THINGS OF YOU, JUST LIKE HE DOES OF SHU-SAN.
GUESS SO.
THAT'S PROBABLY WHAT HE TOOK ME IN FOR, AND ALL.

But I'm not interested.

I'm not gonna wear a gray suit every day like my brother...
...and live in that straight-laced old men's world.

キャーーッ
SQUEAL
KURANO-SUKE!!
I can't even imagine myself in that life.

tmp tmp tmp tmp tmp
KURANO-SUKEEEE!!
UNLIKE YOUR SCHOOLS, MINE IS A SERIOUS—
CONGRATULATIONS!
I KNEW YOU COULD DO IT!
MAKE LOVE TO ME!
LET ME LICK YOUR SHOES!
CALM THE HELL DOWN!
DASH
GAH, WHAT A PAIN.
Aw!
tmp tmp
ZHOOP
MORNING!
CONGRATULATIONS!
THAT'S OUR KURANOSUKE!
THE BOYS, TOO?!
HEY! TAKE YOUR SEATS!
TIME FOR HOMEROOM!
CLATTER
LET GO!
THIS IS CREEPY!

CULTURE FESTIVAL カ
skritch
RIGHT.
OKAY, GUYS.
IT'S ABOUT TIME YOU DECIDED WHAT OUR CLASS IS DOING FOR THE CULTURE FESTIVAL AT THE END OF THE MONTH!
Aw, what a pain!
HEY, KOI-BUCHI!
MY REPORT GOT YOU INTO COLLEGE.
HUH ?!
YOU KNOW WHAT THAT MEANS ...
THE TEST TAKERS ARE ENTERING THEIR FINAL STRETCH!
YOU MAKE SURE NO BURDEN FALLS ON YAMADA, SAWAI, YOSHIKAWA, OR MUKODA—THEY'RE GOING TO INCREASE OUR ADMISSION RATE INTO TOKYO UNIVERSITY!
The Crew Studying for Tokyo U.
Yamada
study study
ガリガリ
Sawai
study study study
ガリガリガリ
Yoshi-kawa
study study
ガリガリ
Mukoda
SO YOU GUYS ON THE RECOMMEN-DATION CREW DO ALL THE FESTIVAL PLANNING, PREP, AND GRUNT WORK ON THE DAY OF!
The Recommendation Crew (Attractive Flirts)
YES, SIR...

WELL?
WHAT SHOULD WE DO?
LET'S PICK SOMETHING EASY.
THIS IS SUCH A PAIN.
IS "NOT" AN OPTION?
CLASS B IS DOING A CAFÉ.

WITH SOME KOIBUCHI FUNDING, MAYBE WE COULD DO A CLUB.
Get a disco ball, a turntable...
BLECH, SOUNDS LAME.
We can just go to an actual club.
THEN LET'S JUST DO THE CLASSIC.
SOFT DRINKS!
LAST YEAR A SENIOR TOLD ME THAT THE EASIEST GIG IS A SOFT DRINKS STAND.

NO EFFORT. I LIKE IT.
PLUS DRINKS WILL SELL WELL, SO WE CAN MAKE MONEY.
OKAY, IT'S A PLAN!

カチャカチャ
chak chak
...
HOW WAS SCHOOL TODAY, KURANOSUKE-SAN?
I ENDED UP IN CHARGE OF A REFRESHMENT STAND FOR THE CULTURE FESTIVAL.
SINCE I GOT INTO COLLEGE.
WELL! THAT SOUNDS FUN!
NOT FUN AT ALL.
JUST WORK.
AND?
WHAT WILL YOU DO?
HMM? JUST SELL CANNED SOFT DRINKS.
We'll have ice.
THAT'S NOT VERY EXCITING.
THEY SAY IT'S THE EASIEST GIG, AND IT'S PROFITABLE.
IT LACKS ANY FLAIR... YOU'RE THE POSTER BOYS FOR TODAY'S LISTLESS YOUTH.
WHY DON'T YOU AT LEAST SELL *SHIRUKO* OR *AMAZAKE*?*
EW, NOT A CHANCE.
You've got old-man tastes.
IN THAT CASE, HOW ABOUT A *TAKOYAKI* STAND, OR A CREPE STAND...?
I'M TELLING YOU, THAT'S TOO MUCH WORK.
GOOD NIGHT!

*A red bean porridge and sweet rice drink, respectively.

KURANO-SUKE-SAN, YOU HAVEN'T HAD DESSERT YET...
SORRY, DON'T WANT ANY! I'M FULL!
stride stride
スタスタ
SLAM
ガタ
skrut
WHAT AM I GOING TO DO WITH HIM?
SHEESH ...
...
strum strum
チャカチャカ
flip
パラ...

glance

COME TO THINK OF IT...
THE DRAMA CLUB ALWAYS DOES SOME SHAKESPEARE OR WHATEVER AT THE CULTURE FESTIVAL...
...

Heh.

THERE'D BE TROUBLE IF THE KIDS AT SCHOOL FOUND OUT HOW MANY DRESSES I HAVE...

screech
KA-CHAK
SORRY TO GET BACK SO LATE.
WELL, WEL-COME HOME.
pat pat

YOU MUST BE TIRED.
LET'S GET YOU SOME DINNER.
HOW'D IT GO?
VERY SMOOTHLY, SIR.

munch munch
ぱくぱく

SAY, SHU-SAN, WHAT DID *YOUR* HIGH SCHOOL CLASSES DO FOR THE CULTURE FESTIVAL?
I CAN'T REMEMBER...
CULTURE FESTIVALS? WHY?

KURANO-SUKE-SAN SAYS THEIRS IS COMING UP SOON.
OH.
I SEE...

I WENT TO AN ALL-BOYS SCHOOL, SO...
...IF I RECALL CORRECTLY...
FRESHMAN YEAR WE DID AN UDON NOODLE STAND...
SECOND YEAR WAS NOODLES AGAIN... AND THIRD YEAR I WAS TEST PREPPING, SO NOTHING.
I...
I SEE...

I'M FAIRLY CERTAIN KURANOSUKE-SAN WOULDN'T DO A NOODLE STAND.
I DON'T WANT TO TALK ABOUT HIM ANYMORE.
WELL?

DID KURANO-SUKE GET ADMITTED?
OH! YES, YES HE DID!
THAT'S GOOD.
I'M GLAD.
Phew...
ホッ…

knock knock
コンコン
KURANO-SUKE.

I'M COMING IN.
ka-chak
ガチャ
CON-GRATU-LATIONS.
MOM TOLD ME.
THANKS.
AS OF APRIL, YOU'LL OFFICIALLY BE A COLLEGE STUDENT.

BECAUSE I WANT TO ENTER THE FASHION INDUSTRY.
F-FASHION ...?
WHAT WOULD YOU DO?
gulp...
ANY-THING IS FINE BY ME.
FOR INSTANCE ...
rustle
I COULD BE EDITOR OF A FASHION MAGAZINE...
...OR I COULD HANDLE THE PRESS FOR A BRAND.
WHATEVER I DO, GOING TO A GOOD COLLEGE DOESN'T EXACTLY HURT MY CHANCES.
SO I DO PLAN TO GRADUATE FIRST.
ANYWAY, WHAT'S THE HARM?
FASHION, THOUGH? DO YOU REALLY THINK DAD WILL...
...L-LET YOU?
WE'VE MANAGED TO STAY A POLITICAL FAMILY FOR GENERA-TIONS...
OH, I'M SURE HE'LL SAY NO.
THE FAMILY HAS *YOU.*
YOU'VE GOT THE GLASSES, THE SIDE PART... YOU'RE THE VERY PORTRAIT OF A POLITICIAN.

BUT I'M GOING TO DO WHAT I WANT. FOR MY SAKE AND MY MOM'S.

BECAUSE I KNOW I INHERITED THIS FROM MOM.

IT'S HER GENES IN ME, HER LOVE OF BEAUTIFUL THINGS.

学園祭
KURA-NOSUKE! WE'VE GOT TROUBLE!

Sign: School Festival

WHAT?

JUST LOOK. YOUR FANGIRLS FROM OTHER SCHOOLS ARE STORMING THE GATE.

KURANOSUKEEEEEE!

ぎゅう ぎゅう SQUEEZE SQUEEZE

WHICH REFRESH-MENT STAND IS KURANO-SUKE'S?!

SO, THOSE DRINKS...
HOW MANY DID YOU BUY?
UH, NOT THAT MANY...
WE'LL SELL OUT IN TEN MINUTES.
SOUNDS GOOD! LET'S SELL EVERYTHING IN TEN MINUTES, AND THEN GO HAVE FUN!
NO, WAIT.
I JUST HAD AN AMAZING SALES IDEA.
gleam
HUH?!
I have a bad feeling...

I DON'T WANT TO DO THIS...
KURANO-SUKE!
DO IT!
WE'LL USE THE PROFITS TO GO TO A HOSTESS CLUB PRE-TENDING TO BE COLLEGE STU-DENTS!
500円
Hug

dun dun
da-dun
ドドドンドン

SHRIEK!!

NEXT IN LINE!
OKAY, PEEL HER OFF.
IT'S THREE SEC-ONDS PER PERSON.
THOSE ARE THE RULES, MISS.
Noooooo!

HOW MANY SO FAR...?
FIFTY!!
drained
LOOK AT THESE SALES!

THIS IS LIKE SHAKING HANDS WITH VOTERS ON THE CAMPAIGN TRAIL...
KURANO-SUKE!!
I knew it... I can't be a politi-cian...
TMP TMP TMP

キラキラーン
GLEAM
HUG ME!!
ひっ
EEP!
むぎゅっ
GLOMP
STOP... C-CAN'T BREATHE!
KURA-NOSUKE, I HAVE SOME BAD NEWS.
HUH? WHAT IS IT?
click
SHE BOUGHT TEN CANS...
...SO SHE GETS A THIRTY-SECOND HUG.
!!!
squeeeeze
WHAT?
WE CAN DO THAT?
wuzza
ザワ
I'LL BUY TEN TOO, THEN!
I'LL TAKE TWENTY.
I'M BUYING 100!!
OKAY, GO GET MORE DRINKS!!

NO GOOD. TIME TO RUN.
SORRY... GOTTA... BATH-ROOM...
HUH?!
DON'T YOU DARE RUN AWAY!
GUYS, ONE OF YOU GO ALONG AND GUARD HIM.
IS THIS ANY WAY TO TREAT A FRIEND?!
DON'T RUN.
I'M NOT GONNA RUN!
Keep the Bathroom Clean
BANG!!
BUT I'M TOTALLY GONNA RUN...
ZHOOP
UP I...
...GO!
WAH!
crash
gasp
EEP!
kshh
HMM?
floof

WHOA...
YOU STARTLED ME.
演劇部
OOPS ...
YOU'RE IN THE DRAMA CLUB?
OH! YES!
Sorry I scared you.
I'M A FRESHMAN!
...
Cuff: Drama Club
lurch
SORRY, BUT YOU NEED TO HELP ME!
HUH?!
3-B REFRESHMENT STAND
"Mad Max" Soft Drink Stall
Here
study study study
study study
dun dun
SURE IS LIVELY OUTSIDE.
huff
I SHOULD'VE TAKEN THE DAY OFF AND STUDIED AT HOME.
NO, THE TEACHER SAID WE HAD TO AT LEAST SHOW UP...
HEY, DOES ANYONE GET THIS PHYSICS PROBLEM FROM LAST YEAR'S EXAM?
HMM?
LEMME SEE IT.

tmp tmp tmp tmp tmp
OH, RIGHT. YOU HAVE TO PLUG THIS IN HERE ——— SEE?
I GET IT.
ZHOOP
HEY!!
HAVE YOU SEEN KURANOSUKE?!
...NO?
TMP TMP TMP
TEE-HEE!
IF YOU SEE HIM, CAPTURE HIM!!
OMG!
Where are you?!
I'll pay up, so let me hold youuuuuu-
...
-uuuu!
...
NOISY OUT THERE.
tmp tmp tmp
YEAH...
tat tat tat
ANYWAY...
...THIS FORMULA GOES ...
I GOTCHA.
CLATTER
HMM?
ANOTHER INTRUDER?

...COOL.
THEY CAN'T TELL.
OKAY!
dash
タッ
murmur
ザワッ
This is bliss.

No one realizes it's me.
Not the teachers...
...or my classmates...
Turns out my narrow shoulders mean wearing women's clothes is a breeze.
Who knew?
THIS OPHELIA COSTUME FROM HAMLET...
I THINK I LOOK BETTER IN IT THAN THE HEROINE FROM THE DRAMA CLUB!
HEH HEH.
Oh, hey.
When I get home today...
...I should try Mom's dresses on.

I know they'll look good on me.
Because I look a lot like Mom.
You don't mind, do you, Mom?
I know you treasured those dresses.

But you don't mind if *I* wear them, right?
WHAT...
...ARE YOU DOING?
HMM?
YOU SAID WE WERE GOING TO A FRENCH RESTAURANT AS A FAMILY TO CELE-BRATE MY ADMISSION...
...SO I DOLLED MYSELF UP!
Is there a problem?
I LIKE IT. YOU'RE TOTALLY MY TYPE.
WHY, THANK YOU!
KU... KU... KURA-NOSUKE, YOU...

Princess Jellyfish Vol. 8/End

キラキラーン
GLEAM
HUG ME!!

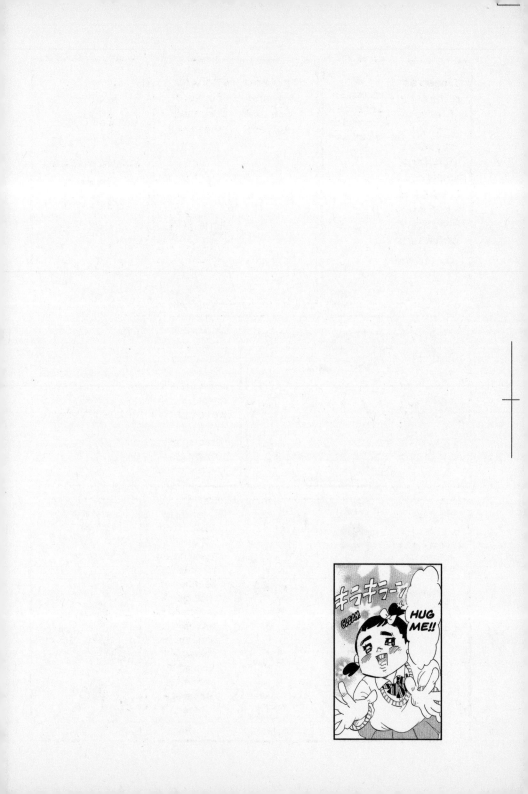

Extra Episode – Princess Jellyfish Bonus Manga

Thank you for your purchase, everyone!!

I'm Akiko Higashimura, the author!!

A revolution recently occurred at Higashimura Pro.

I mean as in the type of "revolution" that happens in Daifugo sometimes.* It was the *Higashimura Pro Digital Revolution.*

Huzzah!

Huzzah!

*A card game.

A while back, in my seventeenth year as a manga artist, I got my very first copy machine for the studio.

It had WiFi scanning capabilities, so we discussed the fact that we could send scans straight to our computers whenever we wanted, which led to the suggestion that we add screen tones digitally during busy times...

By the way, among the assistants in my studio are what I call "the vets": a team of elite, *uber-professional* seasoned veterans...

◦ Wealth of life experience
Have assisted lots of authors

◦ Sociable adults

Engage my editors in friendly conversation

...and a group in their 20s known as "the young'uns."

And among the young'uns are these people...
Sometimes just stares at me.

...who are called the *"Plantlife Team"* (at my instigation) because of their gentle personalities, and always used to get banished to the "TV room," a separate area.

Think of them as the kodama spirits in *Princess Mononoke.*

tee hee
tee hee
WHAT ARE THEY TALKING ABOUT...?
PLANTLIFE TEAM, YOU'RE IN THE TV ROOM AGAIN!!

Somehow, they took my whole production studio digital in a single day.
And so...
taka taka taka taka taka

And that very Plantlife Team...
LISTEN, WANNA TRY DOING SCREEN TONES ON THE COMPUTER?
Not technically on the Plantlife Team.
SHFF
She's female.
HUH?!
THEY CAME OVER HERE ON THEIR OWN INITIATIVE...

Now, on deadline day, their voices echo throughout Higashimura Productions.
S-SAN, I JUST PUT ALL MY CLEANED-UP PAGES ON DROPBOX.
SENDING SCANS!
TETSURO, MAKE A WHITE-LINE LAYER, PLEASE.
I MADE ALL THE SCREEN TONE LAYERS AND THE WORKSPACE IS—
PC

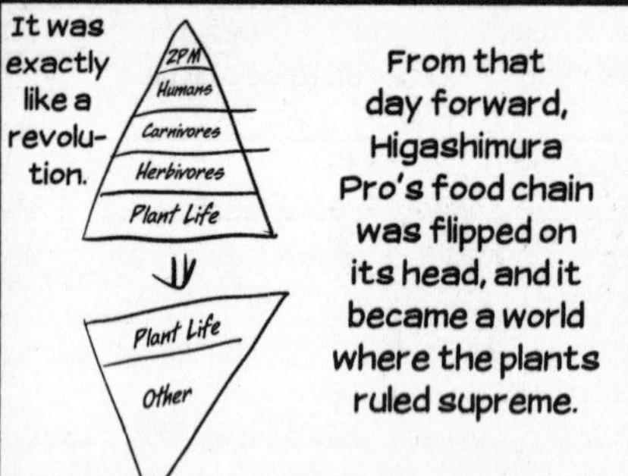
From that day forward, Higashimura Pro's food chain was flipped on its head, and it became a world where the plants ruled supreme.
It was exactly like a revolution.
ZPM
Humans
Carnivores
Herbivores
Plant Life
Plant Life
Other

Which means that during all these "finishing" tasks, the vets can enjoy a nice tea break.
Photoshop data—
Rasterize!!
Rasterize!!
I hear ya!
And after that—
If we want, we veterans can leave all the finishing to the kids and break out the beer early.
Whee! You can do it, guys!
That was the state of Higashimura Pro in late 2015/early 2016.
THEY'RE A DEPENDABLE BUNCH.
HANG IN THERE!
The End

Translation Notes

***The Jellyfish Princess in the Tower*, Page 5**
Disney's *Tangled* was released as *Rapunzel: The Princess in the Tower* in Japan.

***It's been decades since someone new was assigned here.*, Page 11**
In the stereotypical Japanese business model of lifetime employment, instead of firing unwanted employees, companies would transfer them to a dead-end position in an isolated department like this to get them out of the way. Although many people consider this system to be on its way out in Japan's current economy, its effects are still felt and consciousness of it is still strong.

***A used bookstore in Jimbou*, Page 20**
Jimbou, also known as Jimbocho, is often called "Book Town." It's famous for having a large number of used bookstores.

***Suutaro*, Page 34**
This "-taro" is a common Japanese male name ending. Since "Sue" isn't Japanese in the first place, Kuranosuke's attempt to fix the gender of his cover name doesn't exactly make it more believable.

***The Oh and Nagashima Age*, Page 59**
Sadaharu Oh (Chinese name Wang Chen-chih) and Shigeo Nagashima are two of the most famous Japanese baseball players in history. They both played for the Yomiuri Giants during their heyday, and both also later went on to be coaches.

***Isao Hashizume*, Page 139**
Award-winning actor Isao Hashizume, a member of the generation Jiji typically goes for, is famous for such works as *Kitchen*, *Juliet Game*, and a truly spectacular number of TV dramas in various genres.

***Waki Yamato*, Page 140**
Waki Yamato's manga *Asaki Yumemishi* is a retelling of *The Tale of Genji*, the Japanese tale by Murasaki Shikibu which some scholars consider the world's first novel. This traditionally Japanese subject matter is right up Chieko's alley.

***Ain't this Ayano Kongoriki?*, Page 140**
This is a play on the name of actress Ayame Goriki, star of various Japanese TV dramas. She was also the Japanese voice of Mystique in *X-Men: Days of Future Past*.

***Each apartment has a 6-tatami room and a 3-tatami one.*, Page 144**
In Japan, the size of a living area is generally given as how many straw tatami mats could fit into the room, instead of as square feet or square meters. This rule applies even to rooms which don't actually contain any tatami mats. Although these mats have come in different sizes over time, the rough rule of thumb is that 1 tatami mat = 1.6562 square meters. As for the clothes-drying equipment Chieko goes on to mention, this is important because although most Japanese families use washing machines, it's far more common to line-dry clothes by hanging them at the window than it is to use an electric dryer.

***BS is airing a travelogue about Three Kingdoms-related sites.*, Page 158**
This "BS" station is probably BS Asahi, a Japanese satellite broadcasting station.

"Kurage" local bar, Page 166
The actual work Clara uses is "snack," an English word adopted into Japanese to mean a very small bar, usually run by one owner-proprietor, often located near suburban train stations so customers can visit on the way home from work. Some snacks only allow regulars in.

New Year's Cash, Page 173
The Japanese custom is to give money to your own children and the children of relatives and close friends each New Year's. There's no hard and fast rule for what ages of children should get these gifts or how much the gifts should be. A fairly common age range is elementary school through high school. A 13-year-old might get about ¥5,000 from her parents and an additional few thousand yen from each close relative, although the amounts vary. New Year's money is usually placed in a special decorative envelope sold especially for the purpose.

Sweets-Brained Girls, Page 173
Since Banba herself is a girl with sweets on the brain a large percentage of the time, you may wonder why she's regarding these "sweets-brained girls" as almost another species. The Japanese term "sweets-brained" is derogatory online slang for the type of girl or woman who (at least according to the person using the phrase) mindlessly follows every fad promoted by the media. It origin is usually cited as coming from a media trend in the mid-2000s where magazines and ad campaigns targeting a female demographic used the English word "sweets" to refer to desserts and sweet snacks, rather than using any of the words in regular use at the time. So when someone wants to insult what they perceive as "the type of girl who starts using the English word 'sweets' just because the media told her to," they call her "sweets-brained." Hence Banba's "I'm an anthropologist in another culture" attitude to the people in this café—no one would ever call Banba "sweets-brained," just as Banba would never think to call any of her favorite foods "sweets" just because some magazines started doing so (if she even noticed those magazines in the first place). Kuranosuke, of course, is perfectly aware of these trends and plays the role of "sweets-brained girl" whenever he thinks it'll give him a social advantage.

Strangers shouldn't ask Yosui Inoue-type questions like that., Page 176
Born in 1948, Yosui Inoue is a singer-songwriter who known for his sometimes-surreal lyrics. Perhaps to Banba, the question of what clothes she wants is as incomprehensible as surrealist poetry.

Amars' Feast, Page 201
The format "___'s Feast" is a go-to for Japanese titles to films produced overseas. International films with Japanese names in this pattern include: the 1998 French film *Le Dîner de Cons* (which we mentioned in the Volume 11 notes), the 1987 Danish film *Babettes gæstebud* (also known in English as *Babette's Feast*), and the 2015 American film *Love the Coopers*.

A Sukiyaki Feast?, Page 203
Sukiyaki is a lavish meal in Japan, which is why Chieko wanted to make it for Tsukimi, since it's a great celebratory dish. Like hotpot dishes, it features a variety of separate ingredients cooked together at the table, the difference being that a soup base isn't involved. Ingredients are cooked in a sauce whose main ingredients are soy sauce, brown sugar, and sake and/or rice wine. While its hotpot relatives can use many different cuts of meat, in most regions of Japan you're definitely supposed to use beef for sukiyaki, *not* pork, and especially not chopped pork! You get more leeway to choose your non-meats, with a few common choices being tofu, napa cabbage, and shiitake

mushrooms. Many people also dip the cooked beef in raw egg before eating it, which is why Kuranosuke requests an egg later in this scene.

You've got a vibe like that laid-back sunglasses guy from The Alfee., Page 204
Masaru Sakurai, the bassist for the three-member Japanese folk rock band The Alfee.

The combination of beef and shirataki is unbeatable., Page 206
Shirataki are thin noodles made out of the bulbous part of the konjac plant (also known as *konnyaku* and "devil's tongue"). They are an extremely common ingredient in sukiyaki.

Weddings and bloodstains and kekkon, oh my!, Page 238
The Japanese words for "bloodstain" and "marriage/wedding" are homophones spelled with different kanji. They are both pronounced *kekkon*. Since of course it makes no sense for Amars to talk about marriage, Mayaya and Banba assume Tsukimi must gasping "*kekkon*" because she saw bloodstains outside. They immediately leap to the conclusion that someone has been murdered.

Shibuo Kakita, Page 240
The family name Banba chooses, "Kakita," means "persimmon field." Nice touch, Banba.

Where did you get that ring? It looks brilliant enough for Shi Huangdi!, Page 243
Shi Huangdi, born Ying Zheng, was the first emperor of a unified China. His Qin Dynasty ruled a few hundred years before Mayaya's beloved Three Kingdoms period—and given the name "Three Kingdoms," it's no spoiler to say that Shi Huangdi's unification of China didn't last—but no scholar of Chinese history could fail to know of him. He is both famous and infamous, so it's an open question whether Tsukimi should take Mayaya's assessment of the ring as a compliment.

The Dangerous Lives of Koibuchi Boys, Page 261
Peter Care's 2002 film *The Dangerous Lives of Altar Boys* was released as *Innocent Boys* in Japan, making the literal title of this chapter "Innocent Koibuchi Boys."

Jellyfish generals?, Page 266
There's a certain method to Mayaya's madness when she says that jellyfish are "like Warring States generals who come of age and just keep changing names." Generals and other warriors in both China and Japan's respective Warring States Periods tended to have multiple names throughout their lifetimes, and this fact about Japan's Warring States Period is something that all Amars would know from their school days. Men in the Warring States Period would generally be given a name at birth to use until they came of age, and then their proper adult name when they came of age. That's a minimum of two personal names right there! And to make things more complicated, because the Warring States involved a lot of both strategic and forced alliances between different clans, it was common for someone's family name to change as well, for instance when a warlord favored them or when they were adopted into a different family. They might even change all or part of their personal name in deference to a new leader or as an homage to a respected mentor. Then there were the times when they changed family names to make themselves sound more impressive. I could go on, but you get the idea. The shogun we know as "Tokugawa Ieyasu" had these names during his lifetime: Matsudaira Takechiyo, Matsudaira Motonobu, Matsudaira Motoyasu, Matsudaira Ieyasu, and finally Tokugawa Ieyasu. And that's not even counting his various nicknames before and after his death!

Red Arrow, Page 269
The Red Arrow is an all-reserved-seat limited express train operated by Seibu Railway. Banba could board it at Ikebukuro and have a nice trip to Chichibu, a city in Saitama Prefecture.

Jounetsu Tairiku, Page 282
Jounetsu Tairiku is a Sunday night documentary show that began running in 1998. The people or groups documented work in a wide range of fields.

I just skipped the line., Page 303
Almost all Japanese high school students who want to go on to college have to take entrance exams for the colleges they're interested in, and they'll be admitted or not admitted based almost entirely on their scores. The basis for much of this chapter is that Kuranosuke "skipped the line" by getting into his college of choice without taking this exam. W.U. agreed to take him on the strength of recommendation letters, so he didn't have to personally demonstrate his intelligence. This is why he keeps downplaying everyone's congratulations.

Why don't you at least sell shiruko or amazake?, Page 305
Koibuchi is showing his "old-man tastes" here. *Shiruko* is a soupy dessert of mochi and red beans, and while *amazake* literally means "sweet sake," it's actually a non-alcoholic or very-low-alcohol (>1%) fermented rice drink, perfectly appropriate for a refreshment stand. It's sweet with a milky white appearance. Of course, apparently Higashimura-sensei's son Gocchan has old-man tastes, since we saw in Volume 15 that he loves *shiruko*...

I mean as in the type of "revolution" that happens in Daifugo sometimes., Page 327
Daifugo is a Japanese card game. When someone plays four or more cards at once to trigger the "revolution" rule, the value of all non-joker cards is reversed. Pretty much exactly what you see Higashimura describe happen to her "food chain" on the next page.

Think of them as the kodama spirits in Princess Mononoke., Page 327
The kodama are passive tree spirits in Hayao Miyazaki's 1997 film *Princess Mononoke* who chitter without forming recognizable words. You know you want plenty of these benign spirits around in any healthy forest, but to a human they don't seem very exciting, and you can't possibly hope to know what they are saying.

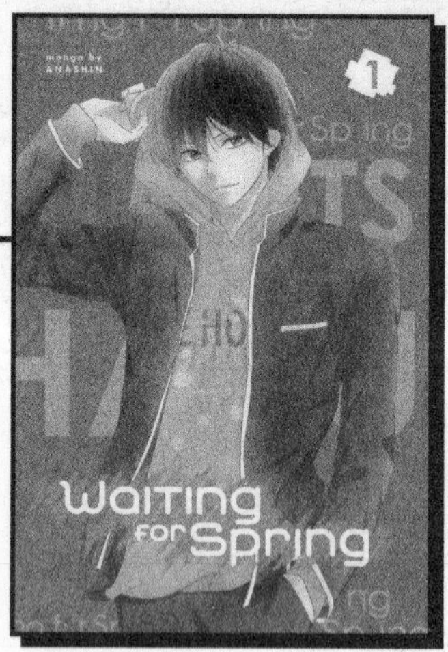

WAITING FOR SPRING

A sweet romantic story of a soft-spoken high school freshman and her quest to make friends. For fans of earnest, fun, and dramatic shojo like *Kimi ni Todoke* and *Say I Love You*.

© Anashin/Kodansha, Ltd. All rights reserved.

KISS ME AT THE STROKE OF MIDNIGHT

An all-new Cinderella comedy perfect for fans of *My Little Monster* and *Say I Love You*!

© Rin Mikimoto/Kodansha, Ltd. All rights reserved.

LOVE AND LIES

Love is forbidden. When you turn 16, the government will assign you your marriage partner. This dystopian manga about teen love and defiance is a sexy, funny, and dramatic new hit! Anime now streaming on Anime Strike!

© Musawo/Kodansha, Ltd. All rights reserved.

KC KODANSHA COMICS

YOUR NEW FAVORITE ROMANCE MANGA IS WAITING FOR YOU!

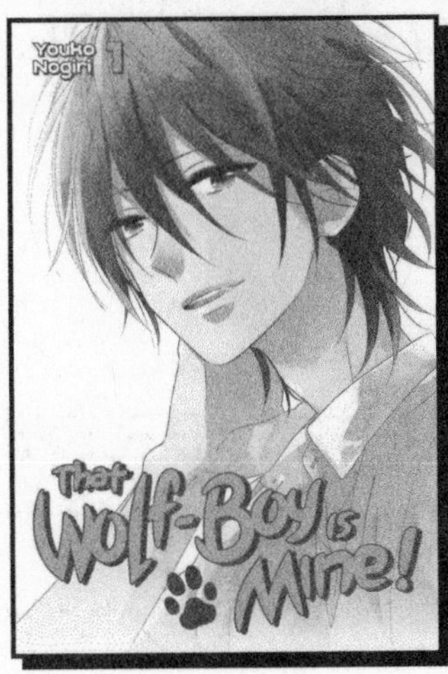

THAT WOLF-BOY IS MINE!

A beast-boy comedy and drama perfect for fans of *Fruits Basket*!

"A tantalizing, understated slice-of-life romance with an interesting supernatural twist."

- Taykobon

© Yoko Nogiri/Kodansha, Ltd. All rights reserved.

WAKE UP, SLEEPING BEAUTY

This heartrending romantic manga is not the fairy tale you remember! This time, Prince Charming is a teenage housekeeper, and Sleeping Beauty's curse threatens to pull them both into deep trouble.

© Megumi Morino/Kodansha, Ltd. All rights reserved.

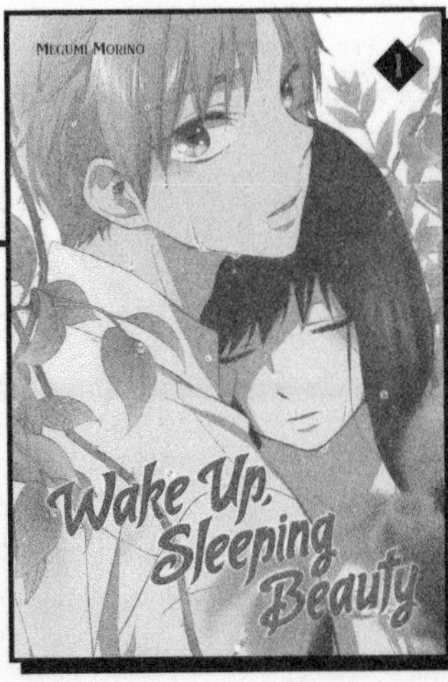

DISCOVER YOUR NEW FAVORITE FANTASY WITH TWO NEW TANTALIZING SERIES!

LAND OF THE LUSTROUS

A BEAUTIFULLY-DRAWN NEW ACTION MANGA FROM HARUKO ICHIKAWA, WINNER OF THE OSAMU TEZUKA CULTURAL PRIZE!

Kigurumi GUARDIANS

LILY HOSHINO, THE BELOVED ARTIST BEHIND *MAWARU PENGUINDRUM*, OFFERS HER CUTE AND TWISTED TAKE ON THE MAGICAL GIRL GENRE!

KC KODANSHA COMICS

In a world inhabited by crystalline life-forms called The Lustrous, every gem must fight for their life against the threat of Lunarians who would turn them into decorations. Phosphophyllite, the most fragile and brittle of gems, longs to join the battle. When Phos is instead assigned to complete a natural history of their world, it sounds like a dull and pointless task. But this new job brings Phos into contact with Cinnabar, a gem forced to live in isolation. Can Phos's seemingly mundane assignment lead both Phos and Cinnabar to the fulfillment they desire?

© Haruko Ichikawa/Kodansha, Ltd. All rights reserved.

Hakka Sasakura's life is about to turn upside-down. She comes home from a day of admiring her student body president to discover that a mysterious creature resembling a man in an animal suit has taken up residence her home. What's more, she has been chosen to work with this strange being to fight off invaders from another dimension and save the world...and she has to kiss him to do so?!

© Lily Hoshino/Kodansha, Ltd. All rights reserved.

KC
KODANSHA COMICS

The award-winning manga about what happens inside you!

"Far more entertaining than it ought to be... what kid doesn't want to think that every time they sneeze a torpedo shoots out their nose?"
–Anime News Network

Strep throat! Hay fever! Influenza! The world is a dangerous place for a red blood cell just trying to get her deliveries finished. Fortunately, she's not alone...she's got a whole human body's worth of cells ready to help out! The mysterious white blood cells, the buff and brash killer T cells, even the cute little platelets—everyone's got to come together if they want to keep you healthy!

Cells at Work!

はたらく細胞

By Akane Shimizu

© Akane Shimizu/Kodansha Ltd. All rights reserved.

Princess Jellyfish volume 8 is a work of fiction. Names, characters, places, and incidents are the products of the author's imagination or are used fictitiously. Any resemblance to actual events, locales, or persons, living or dead, is entirely coincidental.

A Kodansha Comics Trade Paperback Original.

Princess Jellyfish volume 8 copyright © 2015, 2016 Akiko Higashimura
English translation copyright © 2018 Akiko Higashimura

All rights reserved.

Published in the United States by Kodansha Comics,
an imprint of Kodansha USA Publishing, LLC, New York.

Publication rights for this English edition arranged through Kodansha Ltd., Tokyo.

First published in Japan in 2015, 2016 by Kodansha Ltd., Tokyo,
as *Kuragehime* volumes 15 & 16.

ISBN 978-1-63236-563-7

Icon design by UCHIKOGA tomoyuki & RAITA ryoko (CHProduction Inc.)

Printed in the United States of America.

www.kodanshacomics.com

9 8 7 6 5 4 3 2 1

Translation: Sarah Alys Lindholm
Lettering: Carl Vanstiphout
Additional Layout: Belynda Ungurath, Paige Pumphrey, Phil Balsman
Editing: Haruko Hashimoto
Kodansha Comics Edition Cover Design: Phil Balsman